BETJEMAN IN IRELAND

BETJEMAN IN IRELAND

Dominic Moseley

SOMERVILLE PRESS

Somerville Press Ltd,
Dromore,
Bantry,
Co. Cork, Ireland

First published 2023

Designed by Jane Stark.
Typeset in Adobe Garamond Pro
seamistgraphics@gmail.com

ISBN: 978-1-8382544-3-8

This trifle is dedicated to Marzena
who bore my literary travails with
patience and encouragement.

CONTENTS

Foreword 9
Introduction 14
A Sense of Place 28
Betjeman in Love 41
On the Slow Train 58
Undercover in Dublin 61
The Palace Bar 89
The Gothic Revival 101
How to Get On in Society 120
Ireland in Verse 137
Envoi 154
Bibliography 156
Acknowledgements 157
Picture Credits 158

FOREWORD

It is the task of the amateur literary historian to reduce and digest a large amount of material into a comprehensible narrative. In the case of this short work about John Betjeman's connections with Ireland, the source material is extensive and digressive; Betjeman had a wide acquaintance and many different interests. Scholars far abler than I have amply fed on the bones of Betjeman. This is not a work of scholarship; it is what Graham Greene would have described as an entertainment.

I have tried to focus specifically on Betjeman the man, his time in Ireland from his first visit when he was an undergraduate at Oxford through his time as British Press Attaché in Dublin during the Second World War, and several visits after the war, although to make sense of his life in Ireland, on occasion necessitates a net more widely flung.

In particular I will refer in passing to aspects of his life in England which are relevant to this; his love of Victorian buildings, his High Church Anglicanism, his conflicts of personal loyalties, his poetic influences, and his sense of his social status; forever on the arduous ascent between trade and gentry. I have not recounted his life outside Ireland in any detail, except by way of context, as this is not my remit.

Where possible I have let the Poet Laureate speak for himself and have taken the liberty of quoting extensively from his poetry and letters, with grateful thanks to the holders of the copyright of these who indicated to the publisher that I might do so. Betjeman's own words bring his character to life with a warmth which no analytic attempt could do.

I was delighted to be offered this commission as I have enjoyed John Betjeman's poetry for more than five decades although, by some unaccountable omission, they were not included in the syllabus when I read English at Trinity College Dublin.

Having known the faded grandeur of the cavernous dining room of the Kildare Street Club before it was sold to the French government, the Shelbourne before its extensive re-furbishment, the Palace Bar, still *deo gratias*, mostly un-furbished (although it cringingly describes itself as a "Victorian heritage pub"); it was a pleasure to revisit all these places in memory as I did research for this brief monograph.

But the minutiae of much secondary material relating to the extended family history of people he met in Ireland, which might otherwise resemble Burke's *Irish Landed Gentry*, or of poets he was influenced by but who were long dead, have been omitted. However this is exhaustively documented elsewhere in two excellent biographies, as is the majority of his life, spent in England.

Two helpful critics suggested that I completely re-write the book as a chronological narrative; this might be quite good advice but it would be a very different book. A simple chronological account would be rather tedious as it would be a calendar of John

Betjeman's visits to Ireland, but more, it might fail to bring to life the character of the man and his interaction with a country of which he was so fond, in a way particular to Betjeman.

John Henry Newman, ever a helpful guide, counselled aspiring writers not to allow any idea, however good, impede the force of the narrative. Narrative in the case of *Betjeman In Ireland* being sparse, I have lamentably failed to observe the sainted Cardinal's dictum; indeed, this whole book is a series of digressions and diversions and has more meanders than the eponymous river.

I have instead organised the story of Betjeman and Ireland around a few key themes. In order to understand these themes selectivity means an opinion is proffered, but such is the hazard and pleasure of the amateur historian. Few, I hope, will take issue with these, and most of the people concerned, who might take umbrage, are no longer with us. A drawback of this approach is that as we meet the dramatis personae their roles are not always immediately clear but patience will, in due course, be rewarded, albeit with a small amount of necessary repetition.

I have not dwelt at any length on his childhood, unhappy schooling, forays into homosexuality, depression, fear of death; this story is a simpler one; what made Betjeman so fond of Ireland. In doing so we might hope to become familiar with some aspects of Betjeman's complicated character. With that we must dwell a little on his curious marriage to Penelope, whose parents tried to prevent their daughter, raised in an Indian palace, marrying a penniless middle-class scribbler, and his relationships outside his marriage, including several Irish love affairs both requited and unrequited, and in particular his relationship lasting half his adult life with Lady Elizabeth Cavendish.

I have adopted the convention of using contemporary descriptors such as "Eire" or "The Emergency" only in quoted speech and documents but otherwise used accepted modern terms such as Ireland or the Second World War.

The Second World War is a long time ago and a brief description of the context of this time as it relates to the two plus years Betjeman spent in wartime Dublin might provide a helpful context. This is covered in the section entitled "Undercover in Dublin", with some additional material in the section "On the Slow Train".

Likewise, the twilight of the Anglo-Irish Ascendancy has now become permanent night so a canter through nine centuries of Irish history to explain who they were and why is covered in the relevant chapter, particularly for the benefit of those with no more than a nodding acquaintance with Irish history.

In the normal course of compiling a book such as this, part of the pleasure for the author lies in researching the archives of contemporary journals and newspapers and, most pertinently for this work, visiting the places and houses that were familiar to Betjeman in his many trips around Ireland, and, where possible talking to the family, if they still live there. Alas, this was written in the time of the great pandemic when both toll roads and bohreens were closed to travellers. Attempts to talk to the denizens of the few castles still owned by the same families were largely unsuccessful. So, most of the research was based on telephone conversations, exchanges of emails, and the internet; not always the most reliable source of information, or on the more reliable books cited at the end of this work.

My thanks to all those who offered encouragement and advice, in particular to Andrew and Jane Russell of Somerville Press, who invited me to write this book, Jane Stark, typesetter and book designer, Sheila Corr for advice on picture research, Patrick Hickey, friend and author, Thomas McCarthy who gave invaluable advice, Charlotte Mosley, Leo Keohane who helped track down out of print books, Mary Leland, Robert O'Byrne and many others whom I used to test thoughts and ideas. Gerald Dawe was also kind enough to read the manuscript and made many suggestions which I have incorporated in the text. Thanks also to the Betjeman Society who were kind enough to respond with enthusiasm.

All omissions and errors are, of course, the fault of the author; *mea culpa*.

Dominic Moseley,
West Cork 2021

INTRODUCTION

Our story begins with a teddy bear. When John Betjeman arrived at Magdalen College Oxford, he was accompanied by his teddy bear, Archibald Ormsby-Gore, and the bear accompanied him on all his travels until his demise. Archibald must have crossed the Irish Sea with the British & Irish Steam Packet line more often than most teddy bears. Letters from Betjeman were sometimes signed by Archie and often included a sketch of the bear. Evelyn Waugh, for some time a good friend of Betjeman, borrowed the teddy bear for Sebastian Flyte in his great novel of aristocracy, alcoholism and Catholic conversion, *Brideshead Revisited*.

When Betjeman went up to Oxford in 1925, the child of a middle-class London family, who had obtained a place at Magdalen College with some difficulty, he met a gilded circle of the upper classes. Mostly educated at Eton and just young enough to have missed active service in the Great War, centuries of breeding, landed estates and a destiny as rulers of a vast Empire, gave them a self-confidence which would last through the heady decades up to the Second World War.

Those who were from the Anglo-Irish Ascendancy (of whom

more later) may have been rather less sure of their future in the three-year-old Irish Free State, but they continued to lead a life of great privilege. All that a young John Betjeman could offer as the price of admittance to the charmed circle was a talent to amuse and entertain, qualities which he possessed in abundance.

The teddy bear makes another appearance when the poet reaches the age of 50, reminding him of his mortality, although he still had nearly three decades left to live:

> The bear who sits above my bed
> More agèd now he is to see,
> His woollen eyes have thinner thread,
> But still he seems to say to me,
> In double-doom notes, like a knell:
> "You're half a century nearer Hell."

The persona of Archibald fits in with the image most of us have of Betjeman from his later "telly" work; a rumpled, avuncular, tubby figure, always a little threadbare. But there was much more to Betjeman than this faded teddy bear; beneath his comic, self-deprecating exterior was a poet who celebrated every aspect of the idea of love; from fantasy through lust, to agape and self abnegation.

> Kind oer the *kinderbank* leans my Myfanwy,
> White o'er the play-pen the sheen of her dress,
> Fresh from the bathroom and soft in the nursery
> Soap-scented fingers I long to caress

Myfanwy, subject of several of his poetic fantasies, was the wife of his great friend and colleague, the artist John Piper. Betjeman was very fond of both of them but was never to have an affair with

Myfanwy; such was the pattern of his life; unrequited love which he poured out in poetry and love affairs which seldom made an appearance in his verse, except as collateral material. Indeed, the image many of us retain of Betjeman is of his helpless passion for long-limbed tennis players who towered over him, thrashed him set after set, and left him weak at the knees.

John Betjeman, eventually a successful and much-loved poet laureate, was a combination of a self-mocking, comedic talent given to the coining of nicknames for his wife; Penelope (Philth, the Propellor, Plymmi were among his epithets for Penelope), children (his son Paul he named The Egg or Powli and his daughter Candida, Wubz or Wibz), friends and lovers, writing often in Mockney or Cod Oirish, with a man of passionate enthusiasms. His fame of course comes from his poetry, he sold more than a quarter of a million copies of his *Collected Poems* alone in his lifetime and total sales of his poems now exceed two million copies, but his verse springs from his enthusiasms and these will furnish the themes of this work.

Love itself, as we mentioned, was one of his main enthusiasms; the best known of his poems such as "Myfanwy" and "A Subaltern's Love Song", celebrate different aspects of love. The infatuation with strong athletic girls, the childhood infatuations, the sense that all love affairs are doomed to end, the melancholy of "Devonshire St W1" or "Late Flowering Lust". Several writers have suggested that, as a young man, he had various homosexual affairs; he certainly had a succession of female friends, casual and more intimate. This theme is very pertinent to his time in Ireland in poetry and relationships. Not long before his death, he was asked in an interview if he had any regrets; "I wish I had had more sex," he replied.

Above all, Betjeman is known as a poet of place (or a topographical poet for those more critically inclined). So many of his poems are rooted in a sense of place; the Northern suburbs of London, Oxford, the home counties, the wildness of Cornwall. Even a narrative poem such as "The Arrest of Oscar Wilde at the Cadogan Hotel" (a young Betjeman had embarked on a correspondence with the late Wilde's lover, Bosie, and they later became friends) is rooted in a precise sense of place. Betjeman's seven major Irish poems are much concerned with place.

The names of counties drip like honey, the particularity of places, the unique landscape of the Burren. As in many of his poems set in England, so too in Ireland he exalts the neglected, the overlooked midlands, the small towns, Dungarvan in the rain. We will look at these places in his poem-scapes in more detail in the first section of this book.

Not only did he admire the buildings, it gave him great pleasure to stay in the stately homes of his ever-widening acquaintance; Betjeman, an ambitious social alpinist, dearly loved a Lord or a Lady and cultivated them. His wife, Penelope, was the daughter of an ennobled Field Marshal, his mistress for the second part of his life, Lady Elizabeth Cavendish, a daughter of the Duke of Devonshire.

As we shall see, the index to his letters, so beautifully edited by his daughter, Candida, reads a little like a mid-century edition of Debrett's *Peerage* spiced with a good peppering of the Anglo-Irish aristocracy and gentry; unravelling the roots of this Anglo-Irish Ascendancy, from Gaelic clan chieftains, through the Norman Irish, to the Elizabethan and Cromwellian plantations and the fading into obscurity of all of these, poses a tangled skein.

The only significant length of time Betjeman spent in Ireland was during his appointment as Press Attaché to the British Mission from early 1941 to the late summer of 1943, during which he came to know many different aspects of Ireland, particularly the Irish literary and artistic worlds.

The fraught nature of relations between the UK and Ireland made this a more interesting posting than would be usual for such a secondment. Accused of being a British spy, rumoured to have been a target for assassination by the IRA, learning Irish, friendships with Paddy Kavanagh and Jack Yeats, endeavouring to counteract Nazi propaganda, Betjeman's posting to the British Mission was colourful.

In understanding Betjeman, it is important to acknowledge the importance of religion for all his adult life. Brought up with little religion, in his early years he toyed with the Quaker movement before finding his home in high church Anglicanism. He was a regular church goer, including attending Matins and Evensong when he could; he went on at least one Ignatian retreat; he was friendly with several priests, whom he always addressed with the honorific title of "Father" and he enjoyed discussing religion with many of his friends.

He was strongly of the opinion that the Church of England was part of the Catholic church and it caused him distress when his wife Penelope (and some friends) converted to Rome as the implication was that they were no longer in full communion or more seriously that the Church of England was not part of the Catholic and Apostolic Church. His poetry is full of religious references, awe, doubt, fear of death and judgement.

In one of his longest letters to Penelope after her conversion, John Betjeman writes of how much he loves her, wishes they could spend time together on their own, that he had felt jealous of their children because they took her attention away from him, that their time in Ireland had placed strains on their marriage, and most of all how hurt he was by her conversion. He saw this as a direct challenge to his deeply held Christian faith; "It's no good my just saying this. But I do mean it. If I could be with you alone – just you and me alone once a week for a whole afternoon including lunch and tea, I'm sure I should be happy and reasonable again…the difficulty of Wubz [their daughter Candida] being brought up RC is not easy unless I explain to you my fundamental religious longing, which is very difficult. I long for Jesus as a Man, I long to see Him, to be lifted up to Him, to love Him, not to injure Him as much as I do all the time."

One of his best loved poems, "Christmas" concludes with that combination of reverence and uncertainty which was so typical of Betjeman:

Candida Lycett Green (left) unveiling a plaque commemorating her father, John Betjeman, at Marylebone Station in 2006.

And is it true, and is it true,
This most tremendous tale of all,
Seen in a stained-glass window's hue,
A Baby in an ox's stall?
The Maker of the stars and sea
Become a Child on earth for me?

No love that in a family dwells,
No carolling in frosty air,
Nor all the steeple-shaking bells
Can with this single Truth compare –
That God was man in Palestine
And lives today in Bread and Wine

John Betjeman's religious convictions were forceful. In 1963 in a letter to an Anglican priest he wrote: "I absolutely agree with you about fucking about with Methodists, though – another waste of time. No, the C of E is The Catholic Church, tempting though it is to think it isn't – and English Romanism is sectarian".

Despite the forcefulness of his religious opinions his religious faith was never free of doubt. In a letter to his fellow poet, Siegfried Sassoon, written in early 1955, after praising his recently published book of poems, which ask searching questions about the nature of faith, John Betjeman goes on to write, with a candour which we would seldom find nowadays when religion has been banished to the private sphere:

"Never a day goes by without my thinking of my death and the lonely journey into eternity – will it be a journey or will it be blank nothingness... I often wonder whether the Incarnation is true or not. *If* it is, then all is much better. But why should it be? Only those lichened churches you mention tell me that it may be a few good old women and persecuted vicars in country places and hollow-eyed missionaries in towns".

Above all, John Betjeman loved churches; mediaeval churches, Gothic Revival churches, Victorian churches, city and country churches, cathedrals and simple chapels, and abhorred the desecration of attempts to modernise them. His poetry, especially his Irish poems, are full of references to churches, often their ruins; praying in the quiet of a beautiful church, Betjeman achieved momentarily what Coleridge described as the essence of poetry; the willing suspension of disbelief.

When his by then adult daughter, Candida, was to visit Dublin in 1961, her father gave her a list of the places she should see, a list which shows what he found attractive: Merrion Square, the Customs House, the Marino Casino, Henrietta Street, Mountjoy Square, St George's Church, the Rotunda Hospital chapel, the Students' Hospital of the National University, Trinity College Library, City Hall and Parliament House. These and many other places in Dublin of which he was so fond are wonderfully evoked in the programme he made for the BBC in 1979, "John Betjeman's Dublin".

Poet, comic, social climber, lover of women, seeking solace in religion with a flickering faith, there was another side of John Betjeman's character which is seldom written about, not least because he himself kept quiet about it. Partially estranged from his wife, and living most of the week on his own at lodgings in Cloth Fair in the City of London (rented to him by Lord Mottistone, a friend of a friend, perhaps unwisely as John Betjeman or his secretary were later to set the rooms accidentally on fire), he became a visitor to the nearby Bart's hospital.

Every Thursday he would slip out without telling anyone where he was going. Sister Mary Bland, a ward sister at Bart's for more than thirty years, later wrote: "John used to come and have coffee in my room every Thursday morning and then go round and visit the patients in my ward. He was able to make the patients laugh – he was a wonderful mimic... I think because of his horror of death it helped him to see dying patients". He kept in touch with discharged patients and with the families of some who had died, often for several years.

Last, but of course not least, is Betjeman's poetry. This book is not intended as a work of literary criticism or Leavisite analysis but it was poetry which made John Betjeman famous; in his life time he sold more copies of his *Collected Poems* than had predecessors such as Byron or Tennyson sold of their verse in a lifetime despite their undoubted popularity, an astonishing record for a writer described as a minor poet.

In 1958, when the first edition of the *Collected Poems* was published, his lifelong publisher and friend, Jock Murray, was reported as having said: "Reviews have been magnificent. John Betjeman has been given the Duff Cooper Award which was presented by Princess Margaret. Sales are now stabilising at just below a thousand a day. It is now third on the best-seller list in London. What ho! I never remember such a dance since we published Byron's *Childe Harold* in 1812".

His seven specifically Irish poems are quite well known. There are more such as *The Colleen and the Eigenherr* which he omitted from his collected poems. He may be described as a minor poet but he was a master of metre and the apposite word; these poems are the best distillation of all the enthusiasms which animated Betjeman's relationship with Ireland.

He was unusual as a poet in the extent to which he used humour, which is discussed in more detail in the latter parts of this book. He charmed because he appreciated the richness of comedy, of the ridiculous, the bizarre and all his life he loved practical jokes.

James Lees-Milne describes how he and Betjeman used to visit the Geological Museum in Jermyn Street (not one of the most visited tourist attractions in London) and put in new exhibits; an old hazelnut, a pebble picked up in Green Park, with accompanying cards inscribed with complicated descriptions in Latin, placed beside them. "Then we would visit the museum a week or two later to see if our things were still there. They always were." The Museum no longer exists having been swallowed up by the Natural History Museum in Kensington, while Jermyn Street is now a thoroughfare of clothes shops.

Betjeman conceived a strong affection for Ireland on his first visit in 1925 which was reinforced on many subsequent visits; so much so that, like his contemporary and sometime friend, Evelyn Waugh, he thought to buy a house in Ireland. Waugh dallied with the idea of buying Gormanston Castle in Co. Meath, a fine Gothic Revival pile, but changed his mind when he heard that Butlins planned to build a holiday camp nearby. Betjeman's plans too came to naught but his affection for Ireland did not diminish. However, Waugh continued to look for a house in Ireland. In common with several people from modest backgrounds, he thought that by buying a house of substance in Ireland a route might be provided to become part of the Ascendancy.

Waugh wrote to Nancy Mitford: "I think of abjuring the realm and becoming Irish. Do you know anything of Gormanston Castle, for sale? Seat of Lord G. 20 miles from Dublin near the sea.

Gormanston Castle, Co. Meath (JIM FITZPATRICK)

It is advertised as having 'ballroom unfinished' which might be exquisitely romantic. I am going over to see it and perhaps buy it."

"I thought that Lady Gormanston was a young wife who, supposing her husband to have died in the war, married again and had some trouble when he returned in explaining away the pram in the hall and the Teddy Bear on the sofa," she replied. In another letter Waugh wrote "but, in any case, I mean to sell up in England and to emigrate to a Christian country. Liberty, Diversity, Privacy are what I seek. Shall I find them?"

He took the ferry across the Irish Sea and wrote in his diary of the mail boat journey, "the usual passengers, colonels' wives, priests, drunken commercial travellers and this time a number of Jews, presumably tax-evaders."

He described his visit to Gormanston Castle with mixed emotions: "At last the castle which was reached by a back drive through stables and outhouses. It was a fine, solid, grim, square, half-finished block with tower and turrets. Mrs O'Connor, Lord Gormanston's widow, opened the door, young, small, attractive, common.

"She had lit peat fires for our benefit in the main room but normally inhabited a small dressing-room upstairs. The ground-floor rooms were large and had traces of fine Regency decoration. Paintings by Lady Butler everywhere. There were countless bedrooms, many uninhabitable, squalid plumbing, and vast attics. I liked the house; the grounds were dreary with no features except some fine box alleys. The chapel unlicensed and Mrs O'Connor evasive about the chances of getting it put to use again. She gave us all a substantial luncheon. My hirelings drank brandy and seemed disposed to tell funny stories till dusk, but I routed them out and we paraded the wet fields.

"I gave Terence de Vere White my instructions to bid for me at the auction. Then Laura and I went to dine at Jammet's, where we found Billy Wicklow and a BBC pansy at the next table, drank quantities of champagne with them and went to bed quite drunk." Disillusioned by his visit, Waugh wrote: "none of them have servants' bedrooms because at the time they were built Irish servants slept on the kitchen floor. The peasants are malevolent. All their smiles are false as Hell. Their priests are very suitable for them but not for foreigners. No coal at all. Awful incompetence everywhere. No native capable of doing the simplest job properly. No schools for children."

Learning about the impending construction of the Irish holiday camp, Waugh withdrew his bid and in a further letter to Mitford, wrote, "Among countless blessings I thank God for, my failure to find a house in Ireland comes first. Unless one is mad on fox hunting there is nothing to draw one. The houses, except for half a dozen famous ones, are very shoddy in building."

Jammet's (FERGUS O'CONNOR)

The castle was sold to a Dubliner, soon after arrested for smuggling gold, and then sold to the Franciscans who started a school there. They demolished the family chapel, built a bridge between school and castle in the brutalist style which characterised post war ecclesiastic architecture, and have now retreated as their numbers dwindle.

Betjeman's thoughts on Waugh's Irish house buying project were mixed. He wrote to Waugh in 1947:

"Do let me beg you to think twice about settling permanently in Ireland. The physical comforts, the natural scenery, the morality and political outlook of the people is far preferable to those in Britain. But you will always find yourself a foreigner there. Do you mind being a foreigner? Take a lease of a house for three years before you decide."

These themes or enthusiasms, of place, buildings, the Dublin literary world, of people and love, and above all of his poetry, form the structure of this short tribute.

Betjeman was a much-loved poet laureate. Apart from the sales of his poetry he became known to a wider public through his "telly work"; he did not much enjoy this but it was lucrative. When he died it was a significant item of news in the English Press with obituaries in all the national Press and in more distant newspapers such as the *New York Times.*

In the *New York Times* obituary, the writer quoted the words of W. H. Auden on Betjeman: "His poems are slick but not streamlined. He is concerned with actual places. To him a branch railroad is as valuable as a Roman wall, a neo-Tudor teashop as interesting as a Gothic cathedral."

We began with the teddy bear and Sir John Betjeman's life ended with the teddy bear, Archie (Ormsby-Gore). He died at his home in his beloved Cornwall in May 1984. Lady Elizabeth Cavendish, his mistress, wrote to Billa Harrod (with whom Betjeman had also been in love and in a brief engagement mid-way through his engagement to Penelope whom he was to marry): "He died on the most beautiful sunny morning with the sun streaming into the room.... Carole (one of his nurses) was holding one of his hands & me the other & he had old Archy & Jumbo in each arm & Stanley the cat asleep on his tummy".

A SENSE OF PLACE

"Ireland seemed to me Charles Lever and aquatints come true. I thought it was the most perfect place on earth. What I really liked was the Ireland of the Ascendancy, and I particularly liked people who had rather gone to seed," John Betjeman recalls in 1976 five decades after he first visited Ireland.

For most poets, place is unimportant, imaginary or incidental to the thoughts they want to communicate. For example, "The Lake Isle of Innisfree" is a vehicle for Yeats's thoughts in the poem rather than a tangible place; for Coleridge place is invented to create a mythology; for Shakespeare place is only a way of locating the action in history.

There are a few exceptions: Patrick Kavanagh, who became a friend of John Betjeman during the latter's posting to Dublin, wrote: "A gap in a hedge, a smooth rock surfacing a narrow lane, a view of a woody meadow, the stream at the junction of small fields – these are as much as a man can fully experience". Wordsworth was also a poet for whom place was important: "ye knew him well, ye cliffs and islands of Winander", the only one of the Romantic poets for whom this was the case.

W.H. Auden (CARL VAN VECHTEN)

Betjeman knew several contemporary poets well; T. S. Eliot who was briefly a teacher of Betjeman's at his prep school, W. H. Auden, a contemporary at Oxford; both remained friends for many years. Louis MacNeice was at public school with him, Philip Larkin was also a friend; but none of these directly influenced John Betjeman as a poet of place.

In his poetry, brand names are used to tie the verse to time and place: Robertson's Marmalade, Fuller's Angel Cake, Home & Colonial, Star, International while in the Irish poems these yield to the descriptions of the landscape he observes, so often through a mist of rain.

Betjeman's attachment to the particularity of place is strongly evoked in a talk he gave on the BBC Home Service in 1943: "For me, at any rate, England stands for the Church of England, eccentric incumbents, oil-lit churches, Women's Institutes, modest village inns, arguments about cow parsley on the altar, the noise of mowing machines on Saturday afternoons, local newspapers, local auctions, the poetry of Tennyson, Crabbe, Hardy and Matthew Arnold…leaning on gates and looking across fields."

Half a century later, the Prime Minister, John Major, echoed Betjeman in his definition of Englishness: "Fifty years on from now, Britain will still be the country of long shadows on county [cricket] grounds, warm beer, invincible green suburbs, dog lovers, and – as George Orwell said – old maids bicycling to Holy Communion through the morning mist."

Importantly, two of the poets who most influenced John Betjeman were poets fixed in place and in time; the late eighteenth century. One was George Crabbe, a minor poet, now largely forgotten. He wrote in heroic couplets detailed descriptions of provincial and rural life and was admired by nineteenth-century contemporaries. Byron wrote of him that he was "nature's sternest painter, yet the best" but his reputation faded as the Romantics experimented with new ideas as to the nature and purpose of poetry.

The other poet who strongly influenced Betjeman was Oliver Goldsmith. A fine bronze statue of Goldsmith made by J. H. Foley in 1866 stands to the right of the main gate of Trinity College Dublin. John Betjeman wrote to his wife, Penelope, in 1978 six years before his death: "My darling Plymmi… I have just re-read Goldsmith's 'The Deserted Village' which influenced me more than any other English poem. Ernie [his father] used to read it to me always daily, when I was six or seven. I still think it is one of the best English poems and gave me a longing for Ireland from which I have never really recovered."

"The Deserted Village", published 250 years ago in 1771, describes a village, probably Auburn near Athlone, which lay in ruins after its people had left, their land taken, and emigrated to America. Like much of Crabbe's poetry, it is composed in heroic couplets. Although a social commentary on greed and inequality, the sense of place is very particular.

In a letter to C.S. Lewis, an enemy of Betjeman since the time he was his tutor at Oxford, written in December 1939, Betjeman alludes to the influence of a third poet, Spenser, who served the Lord Lieutenant of Ireland in the 1580s and bought an estate near Doneraile: "Spenser's amazing powers of topographical description which are best appreciated when one has visited the neighbourhood of Clonmel, Youghal and Waterford", all places which were dear to John Betjeman but the point he was really making was that these are real places.

John Betjeman was pre-eminently a poet of place. From his first visit to Ireland; at Oxford, among his many friends were several from Ireland who, as we will discuss later (see p. 101) became friends of a lifetime: "Cracky" Clonmore, Pierce Synott (for whom Maurice Bowra nursed an unrequited passion, firmly dispelled when Synott, Bowra and Betjeman made their first visit to Ireland in 1926), Betjeman continued to visit Ireland frequently until the late 1950s, became Patron of the Friends of Monkstown Church in 1974 and made "Betjeman's Dublin" for the BBC in 1979, five years before his death. He lived in Dublin for nearly three years during the Second World War. During this time he travelled extensively around Ireland, by train, by car (when petrol was available), horse and trap, and, notably in one of his Irish poems, by bicycle.

Bowra was a frequent correspondent of John Betjeman's for the rest of his life. Maurice Bowra and "Colonel" Kolkhorst were the doyens of rival academic salons at Oxford when John Betjeman was up at Magdalen. Both were seriously unmarried, as the contemporary euphemism described it, and hated each other bitterly. Bowra was the Warden of Wadham College while Kolkhorst lectured in Spanish. Bowra's reputation rests on his literary criticism and his pithy aphorisms such as "buggery was invented to fill that awkward hour between Evensong and cocktails" quoted by Betjeman in *New Bats in Old Belfries*. While the latter two have suffered a sad decline, the former continues to flourish in the University of Oxford.

Bowra shared Betjeman's enthusiasm for minor poets and encouraged it when Betjeman was an undergraduate, in particular Bowra promoted the poetry of W. B. Yeats in England to a wider audience. The salon of the Colonel (the title was invented by John Betjeman and Denis Kincaid) was rather different; there was a ritual in which the undergraduates consumed several glasses of sherry or Marsala then began to dance around his rooms between the suits of Japanese armour chanting: "The Colonel's drunk". We digress from place but both dons were important influences on the later poetry of John Betjeman.

Dublin he knew well, but he also visited Northern Ireland where he stayed at Clandeboye, the decaying home of his Oxford friend, Basil Ava, the West Coast (Galway and Clare), and at Caledon home to the brother of Field Marshal Lord Alexander of Tunis.

Co. Waterford was among the many Irish counties he visited, staying several times with his mistress, Lady Elizabeth Cavendish, at her family home, Lismore Castle, and visits to Emily Villiers-Stuart near Dungarvan, memorably refrained in the rain in one of his more wistful poems, but chief among the Irish places which captured his affections were the forgotten Midland counties of Ireland; visiting these was convenient on his frequent stays with the Longford family at Pakenham Hall in Co. Westmeath.

Place meant to Betjeman not just the location but the inhabitants, the culture and above all the buildings. So many of his Irish poems include descriptions of ruined estates, mansions and graveyards. His sense of the importance of buildings in landscape in Ireland is conveyed in a letter to Michael Rosse of Birr Castle in 1940 in which he enthuses about the Irish Architectural Records Association of which Betjeman together with Lady Wicklow were founder members and, thinking of the good architecture in Ireland which went on until the 1870s, concludes: "Love to Anne and oh God, to be in Ireland again and happy as we once were".

The words of Betjeman's poems convey much of his enchantment with place during his frequent visits to Ireland.

"The Small Towns of Ireland" is a ballad written in the style of Tom Moore, the eighteenth-century writer chiefly famous for his "Irish Melodies", in which John Betjeman imagines the ballad pinned up on a board in a pub, that also serves as a general shop, among notices for the local Feis and Gaelic football matches. These are the towns "by bards...neglected", towns of ruined mansions and

Clandeboye (ROBERT FRENCH, LAWRENCE COLLECTION, NATIONAL LIBRARY OF IRELAND)

nettle covered graves, towns with their Mall of elegant Georgian houses, of fair days, courthouses and barracks now burned. They are towns of small cabins beneath the prominent new steeple of St Malachy's Catholic Church. John Betjeman describes these towns with warm affection, concluding with the envoi:

> O my small town of Ireland, the raindrops caress you,
> The sun sparkles bright on your field and your Square
> As here on the bridge I salute you and bless you,
> Your murmuring waters and turf-scented air.

His affection for the overlooked parts of Ireland, together with two other notable enthusiasms, is also expressed in a letter to his lover Camilla Russell, written complete with a hand drawn map in August 1931:

"Darling, your letter arrived today just before I was leaving Clandeboye for a delightfully obscure journey through the North of Ireland over the border and into the dear old Free State which is far better. Cavan where I have forty minutes to wait is the scene of the Protestant v. Catholic riots. I hope I shall see some. I am now in a very decayed first-class carriage jolting through Irish landscape with a glimpse now and then through beech trees of an imposing eighteenth-century house with cracked stable and broken windows doubtless the residence of some insane and obscure peer... Poor darling [I want to] give you a terrific kiss on the lips and seal your eyes with two more kisses and take you away to a large and comfortable house in the Irish Free State where we would live in happy madness and sin until we died."

Although a poem bidding goodbye to love, "The Irish Unionist's Farewell to Greta Hellstrom in 1922" is also rooted in place. Greta Hellstrom did not (as far as we know) exist and the poem was not written in 1922 when Betjeman was a schoolboy. He had fallen in love with a young American beauty, Emily Sears, at the time married to Lord Hemphill of Tulira Castle in Galway. The love was unrequited although this was one of the only two of his love attractions which perturbed his wife, Penelope. Emily was to divorce in Reno (divorce was only legalised in Ireland in 1996) and marry Ion Villiers-Stuart of Dromana House in Co. Waterford. The farewell is set in the nearby town of Dungarvan:

Oh! The fighting down of passion!
Oh! The century-seeming pain
Parting in this off-hand fashion
In Dungarvan in the rain.

Dungarvan (MIK HERMAN)

The last line acts as a refrain to each verse, celebrating the often-wet ordinariness of a small town between Cork and Waterford, the statue in the square, the corner boys, the bells of the Angelus, the Comeragh mountains, the ruined house, the sense of heartbreak for unreciprocated love physically rooted in Dungarvan. Happily, Betjeman and Emily remained friends; we find him writing in the 1950s about a recent trip to the cinema in London with Emily.

The small towns of Ireland are the loci of "A Lament for Moira McCavendish", described by Christopher Booker as the most heart-rending poem in the English language. Whether its subject is a thinly disguised allusion to Elizabeth Cavendish or to another of Betjeman's Irish loves need not concern us at this moment; this again is a poem of place. Tallow, the river Blackwater, the musk and potato, the ruined demesne and windowless mansion (seldom absent from Betjeman's Irish poems), Castletownroche, the diesel train. Although the poem is a lament for Moira, his *acushla machree*, (not of course the very much alive Elizabeth Cavendish), it is the feeling for place which frames the poem.

Betjeman returns to the Blackwater in "Ireland's Own" or "The Burial of Thomas Moore" who was buried in Bromham in Wiltshire, but should, the poet writes, have been buried in Ireland, "where the Blackwater glides...or maybe a rath with a round tower near/and the whispering Shannon delighting the ear".

First published under a pseudonym in 1938 in the *Westmeath Examiner*, the most ambitious of John Betjeman's Irish poems is "Sir John Piers". It tells the true story of the "bold, bad baronet" Sir John Piers, a schoolfellow and friend of the patriot Lord Cloncurry, who in 1807 determined to seduce Eliza, Lady Cloncurry, the beautiful young wife of his friend. Cloncurry sued him for Criminal Conversation and won vast damages of £20,000 which ruined Piers. Pursued by his creditors, Piers fled to the Isle of Man where he lived his last years dreaming of his ruined estates in Tristernagh.

The poem begins with a grand picnic, the *fête-champêtre*, on the shores of Lough Ennel (twenty miles from Pakenham Hall, the Longfords' home), a large lake to the West of Mullingar, and the second part, the seduction, is written entirely in terms of the landscape:

> I love your brown curls/ black in rain my colleen,
> I love your grey eyes/ by this verdant shore
> Two Derravaraghs/ to plunge into and drown me
> Hold not these lakes of light/ so near me more

The beech trees roar above Glencara, the exile walks along the beach to Jurby, he looks forward to his return to Lough Iron and his ghost haunts the overgrown, locked graveyard of Tristernagh.

This inspiration of place may have been provided by an occasion on which Betjeman went rowing on Derravaragh with Cathleen

Delaney, an actress at the Gate, with whom he had a brief affair, while they were both staying at Pakenham Hall. The Gate Theatre in Dublin was founded 1928 by Michael MacLiammoir and Hilton Edwards (in Dublin literary circles they were known as Sodom and Begorrah). Lord Longford became chairman in 1930.

The other place which Betjeman loved was also Celtic: Cornwall, where, fulfilling his wish, he died and was buried. Cornwall was the inspiration for several of his poems; there he found the same wildness of nature that so attracted him to the west coast of Ireland. In "By the Ninth Green, St Enodoc" he muses on the angry sea:

On slate compounded before man was made
The ocean ramparts roll their light and shade
Up to Bray Hill and, leaping to invade,
Fall back and seethe.

The most picturesque and probably the best known of Betjeman's Irish poems is "Ireland with Emily" in which the poet imagines and describes bicycling in the West of Ireland with Emily in the war. He begins by painting the scene of a Sunday in the country as the long procession of the devout, all dressed in black, make their way to church then continues evoking the particularity of the midland counties of Ireland, often forgotten compared to the more spectacular west coast:

Bells are booming down the bohreens,
White the mist along the grass,
Now the Julias, Maeves and Maureens
Move between the fields to Mass.
Twisted trees of small green apple
Guard the decent whitewashed chapel,

Gilded gates and doorway grained,
Pointed windows richly stained
With many-coloured Munich glass.

See the black-shawled congregations
On the broidered vestment gaze
Murmur past the painted stations
As Thy Sacred Heart displays
Lush Kildare of scented meadows,
Roscommon, thin in ash-tree shadows,
And Westmeath the lake-reflected,
Spreading Leix the hill-protected,
Kneeling all in silver haze?"

Before moving on to the familiar invocation of ruined demesnes; but then the poem changes pace with the awe-inspiring landscape of the Burren. The Burren is an extraordinary lunar like area of limestone in County Clare, edged by the Cliffs of Moher. It is entirely unlike any other area in these islands and clearly made a strong impression on Betjeman:

Stony seaboard, far and foreign,
Stony hills poured over space,
Stony outcrop of the Burren,
Stones in every fertile place,
Little fields with boulders dotted,
Grey-stone shoulders saffron-spotted,
Stone-walled cabins thatched with reeds,
Where a Stone Age people breeds
The last of Europe's stone age race

I have quoted more extensively from this poem as it explains better than any exegesis might do what attracted John Betjeman to these places. The poem ends with a reprise of the ruined graveyards of the Ascendancy.

Seamus Heaney was equally inspired by the Burren and wrote his poem about a vision in the form of a young woman he imagined in this place. The poem, "Aisling in the Burren" (aisling meaning a spirit or dream poem) is worth reading.

For a poet who loved to root his poems in the particularity of place, Ireland provided ample inspiration. It seemed to Betjeman that Ireland had an atmosphere uniquely its own. Staying at Pakenham Hall in 1931 he wrote to T. S. Eliot: "a silence so deep one hardly dares speak in it and where there is no sound over the hills except at evening where you can hear the turf carts rolling over the bog two miles away… London seems like some mad dream in all this green, wet civilisation."

BETJEMAN IN LOVE

Betjeman's first infatuation, his "first and purest love" as he described it later, was as a small boy in kindergarten in Highgate, North London. He was entranced by the blonde hair and blue eyes of Peggy Purey-Cust with whom he walked to their school, Byron House. Betjeman's father had a successful family business manufacturing furniture. Peggy's father was Admiral Sir Herbert Edward Purey-Cust. In a poem written nearly four decades later in 1954, "False Security", John Betjeman relates the occasion on which he was invited to a children's party at Peggy's home and, on his departure heard her mother ask: "I wonder where Julia found that rather common little boy?"

In England of the early twentieth century, social class divisions were marked, and between the two children attending the same school, one from the manufacturing classes, the other an admiral's daughter, there was a chasm. The same issue would complicate other relationships in Betjeman's life, most notably with his wife, although in time John successfully traversed this ravine.

His apprenticeship in love, aged fifteen, is described by James Lees-Milne in his diary in 1973: "as we drove past Malmesbury,

John said...'In that village I had my first experience of sex, with the son of the Vicar. It was in a punt on the river. I was quite spent. That night the brother came into my room, but I was too shocked by what I had done with the other, during the afternoon, and so lost a second opportunity'".

In *Harvest Bells: Uncollected Poems* published in 2019, "Sweets and Cake" is a poem about two teenage schoolboys, Teddy and Neville, fumbling in bed: "How *could* you squirt / That nasty stuff all down my shirt!" perhaps recalling this early experience in love.

Betjeman described his ideal woman (in terms chiefly of appearance) in a reference to 'Freckly' Jill Menzies, for many years his secretary after the war and with whom he was more than a little in love, in a letter in 1955 to one of his oldest Irish friends, William Wicklow:

"The Mosquito [another life-time friend] was so attracted by my ex-secretary Jill Menzies (turned-up nose, freckles, wide blue eyes, high cheek bones, sulky lips and a boyish figure and very literary and artistic [these latter characteristics at the end of the list] that he said, 'If I lived in the same town as that girl for a fortnight, I'd go normal.'" Patrick Kinross was one of Betjeman's many male friends who was seriously unmarried by disposition, although he did once wed very briefly, a co-habitation which lasted for a year.

By the time Betjeman went to live in Dublin in 1941, he and Penelope had been married for eight years, but their engagement, wedding and marriage had been anything but straightforward. As was mentioned in the Introduction, Penelope had grown up in an imperial palace; her father, Field Marshal Sir Philip Chetwode, was Commander in Chief of the Army of India, in 1933 one of the most important military positions in the world. In the

First World War he had become a hero when the cavalry brigade under his command routed a crack German cavalry regiment, the Prussian Uhlans. Penelope was attractive without being beautiful, an unconventional debutante, who preferred horses to balls, and an avid student of Indian religion and mythology, an interest she retained to the end of her life when she died at the gates of a Hindu temple in the Himalayan foothills in 1985.

Johnnie Churchill, nephew of Sir Winston, was a suitor and she had an affair ("pure physical passion" she later wrote) with Sir John Marshall, more than thirty years her senior, who was head of the Indian Archaeological Service. Then into her life came a third John. Penelope met John Betjeman when she brought some of her Indian photographs to the offices of the *Architectural Review,* where he scraped a living as a journalist.

Clearly, they fell deeply in love as they sat on the floor together looking through the photographs but Penelope's parents, when eventually informed, were horrified. Her mother, Lady Chetwode wrote: "we ask people like that to our houses but we don't marry them".

Penelope was packed off to India, the relationship faltered; during their secret engagement John Betjeman got engaged to at least two other women, and fell in love with Billa Cresswell (later married to the economist, Dominic Harrod) who was to remain a close friend for the rest of his life. Penelope returned to England but was then dispatched by her parents to the South of France to stay with an aunt; eventually John and Penelope married clandestinely.

Chetwode loved his only daughter dearly, and her father was perhaps the greatest love of Penelope's life. For her sake he determined that he must accept John, a penniless journalist and occasional poet from a different social stratum (much to Ernie Betjeman, his father's regret, John was not to be the fourth generation to take over the family business manufacturing ornate furniture), who had failed his Oxford finals.

Maurice Bowra recollected that Chetwode was unsure how John Betjeman should address him; "Sir might be all right but does not seem intimate enough...you can't call me Philip, that wouldn't do. You can't call me Father – I'm not your father. You'd better call me Field Marshal".

In the event, Betjeman, in his comedic and often denigratory style, would refer to his father-in-law, Philip Chetwode, to Penelope and to friends, as "the Woad" with its implications of savage Pictish warriors. Many of the nick-names which John Betjeman constantly invented were not affectionate, including that of his infant son, Paul, referred to as 'the Egg' or later as Powlie, from whom he was estranged until the poet's death.

The marriage of John and Penelope was unconventional as every unhappy family is unhappy in its own way in keeping with Tolstoy's dictum. For many years they had little money, their interests were not at all similar, hers inclined more to Indian mysticism and horses, while his were to Victorian buildings and poetry; John Betjeman had various brief affairs and possibly Penelope had an affair in Germany shortly after they had wed. Penelope was teetotal while her husband enjoyed good wine and whisky, at times in heroic quantities. They shouted at each other, argued continually and eventually Betjeman left her to live with his mistress, Lady Elizabeth Cavendish; normally a kindly man, he treated Penelope as badly as Byron, a poet who had rivalled Betjeman in popularity in his life-time, had treated his wife. Her rather tragic life inspired

Field Marshal Sir Philip Chetwode
(JOHN ST HELIER LANDER)

Mary Alexander to turn it into a charming novel, *Mrs Betjeman*, published by the Paris Press in 2019. The fictionalised account of her affair as a young woman with Sir John Marshall is written with great tenderness.

The original literary Penelope waited twenty years for the return of Odysseus; ten were spent fighting the Trojan Wars, the other ten on the journey home. Even in adverse weather, the sail from Troy to Ithaca would take a few weeks. Much of the return voyage was spent in the arms of the lustful nymph Calypso and later in the bed of the enchantress, Circe. Penelope Betjeman waited in vain; although her husband's letters to Elizabeth in the archives of Victoria University, are hardly passionate, he was clearly enamoured of her and there were no further casual affairs. Not Calypso but perhaps Circe.

Both John and Penelope became increasingly religious; he made the journey from the Quakers to high church Anglicanism while Penelope eventually converted to Roman Catholicism, a final rift between them (and between John Betjeman and Evelyn Waugh, also a Roman Catholic convert and social arriviste, who had proselytised Penelope, but whose enthusiasm for her clearly extended beyond the Catechism. He dedicated his novel about the Empress Helena to Penelope, as well as writing to her in a letter, redacted by his estate, that he was looking forward to "a fine fuck" on her return. Despite all of this, their letters show that John and Penelope Betjeman loved each other until the end of their lives. Penelope always remained loyal to John and supportive of his writing and she was to find their parting, in the latter years of his life, heart-breaking.

I suspect that Betjeman like many others, found the externalities of religion, the buildings, the rituals, the smells and bells, attractive but was less convinced of the eternal verities. In contrast Penelope was on a journey in which she progressively shed the externalities in search of the all important internality.

A poem of Betjeman's which was excluded from the *Collected Poems* by Jock Murray, his lifelong publisher, as being too intimately personal, expressed the anguish he felt when Penelope was received into the Roman Catholic church (this sonnet was sent to his friend the Irish poet Geoffrey Taylor in March 1948):

In the perspective of Eternity
The pain is nothing, now you go away
Above the steaming thatch how silver-grey
Our chiming church tower, calling 'Come to me

My Sunday-sleeping villagers!' And she,
Still half my life, kneels now with those who say
'Take courage, daughter. Never cease to pray
God's grace will break him of his heresy.'

I, present with our Church of England few
At the dear words of the Consecration see
The chalice lifted, hear the Sanctus chime
And glance across to that deserted pew.
In the perspective of Eternity
The pain is nothing, – but, ah God, in Time.

Most of this was in the future when they arrived in Dublin; they already had an infant son, Paul, and a daughter Candida was to be born in Dublin. Betjeman's estranged relationships with his father and later with his own son are not directly pertinent to the title of *Betjeman in Ireland*, and are covered in detail by his two biographers.

In 1938, they had thought of moving to Ireland. In a letter to his mother, John Betjeman wrote: "I have written all that I have written which was worth writing in Ireland, and I regard it as salvation… P likes horses and the country and religion. She will get all three".

To understand some of the important connecting threads in Betjeman's life and his time in Ireland, it is sensible to understand some of the people with whom Betjeman was in love, in addition to Penelope, whether real or imagined.

John Betjeman had already had an affair with Camilla Russell while staying at Pakenham Hall before his marriage. Camilla was the daughter of Sir John Russell, head of police in Cairo. They became secretly engaged in August 1930.

He wrote to Patrick Balfour about his engagement:

"I ought to tell you that I proposed marriage to a jolly girl last weekend and got accepted. It has left me rather dippy. It occurred at two in the morning – suddenly two arms were raised from the floor and put around me… I kissed first the tip of her nose and then the neck and then the forehead and we took off our shoes in order to go upstairs quietly and we turned off the lights and stood on the stone floor of the hall and suddenly two cool little hands were in mine and then a subtly unresisting body pressed against me and I kissed her full on the lips for the first time…. Don't say anything about that engagement business, Patrick. It may come to nothing."

What a wonderful sense of anti-climax. Lady Russell was determined to prove John Betjeman right and forbade Camilla from seeing him. Camilla returned to Cairo where she met Christopher Sykes whom she was to marry, while Betjeman had two new women in his life; Pamela Mitford and Penelope

Chetwode. The upper classes were happy to invest in travel to prevent their daughters marrying John Betjeman.

Pakenham Hall also provided the *mise-en-scène* for another affair in 1938 with Cathleen Delaney, an actress mentioned earlier. Cathleen Delaney was described by Edward Pakenham as a "cross between Helen of Troy and Paddy the Next Best Thing". She wrote to him at Pakenham Hall in 1938: "I can't even bear to think of the weekend after you had gone…it's only your leaving was such a wrench…it's such an awful thought, that in spite of feeling about you the way I do, I haven't the slightest claim on you, not the very least in the world."

Penelope had suggested to Betjeman that they should buy a house in Ireland "because it is so free and easy" before they married. He looked at a few houses but nothing came of it, although he considered it again in 1938, as we have just seen, yet his wife seldom accompanied him on his visits to Ireland in the 1930s which were mainly with his Oxford friends, despite the fact that Penelope enthusiastically adopted most of his friends in the various places where they lived together.

The first infatuation which caused Penelope serious concern, although paradoxically it was one of the few which never became a physical relationship, was with Emily in Co. Galway. Emily Sears was a beautiful American heiress who had been rescued in a riding mishap in the Borghese Gardens in Rome by an Irish peer, Lord Hemphill. They married and went to live in Tulira Castle (the setting of George Moore's *Hail and Farewell*) where the Betjemans went to stay in 1942.

Apart from being the genesis for one of John Betjeman's memorable Irish poems, "Ireland with Emily", quoted in the previous chapter, the visit plunged Penelope into misery.

She wrote: "John absolutely fell for Emily, and I'll never forget the agony of jealousy, the only time I've ever felt jealousy I think, when he stayed up talking to her till about 1.00 a.m. and I went up to bed and he never came in. In point of fact, I needn't have worried a bit; she was already secretly engaged to someone called Ion Villiers-Stuart who lived in a very beautiful and famous house called Dromana which has now been pulled down. I mean, she wasn't in the least in love with John, but he was mad about her. She subsequently married Ion Villiers-Stuart, then he died beside her in bed after two years. She had to get a Reno divorce from Lord Hemphill, because you couldn't get a divorce in Ireland. Ion Villiers-Stuart's wife, too, was an alcoholic, oddly enough; she died, and he married Emily".

Despite Penelope's anxiety this was not to be a relationship which came between John and Philth, as he (affectionately?) addressed his wife. In 1949 (Emily's second husband, Ion Villiers-Stuart was by now dead), John Betjeman wrote:

"Dearest Emily…you know how much I loved your coming up as you did. You know now you need never be lonely. God bless you. My goodness! That scent you put in your hair! Those wet woods! That stream! The sunset behind Dublin church towers! St Anthony pray for us. Dear Emily. Love, John."

Betjeman and Emily remained friends and in the 1970s they are recorded going to the cinema in London together with Penelope, from whom John Betjeman was by then separated, although still in love.

Emily Villiers-Stuart was recalled by the Cappoquin poet, Thomas McCarthy: "as a youth I knew Emily well (in as much as a poor child can know an aristocrat) as we set up a branch library in the old Villiers-Stuart church in Villierstown, at the gates of the estate. We used to have tea together in the kitchen at Dromana. His long relationship with the Duke of Devonshire's sister meant that he knew Lismore Castle very well where I guess he must have met Kick Kennedy. I know the printer Hogan in Lismore printed poems for 'Moira McCavendish' as he called her. Rare and valuable sheets now". We will return to Lismore and the Kennedy family later.

Emily reminisced of her early meeting with Betjeman: "John had a motor-car – no-one then had a motor-car... Well Penelope went off in the car straight away to look for a Connemara pony. So John and I had nothing but bicycles, and we went on the ride John describes in 'Ireland with Emily'. I said the nicest place we could go was where the St George family lived. John was thrilled with them, because they were rather aristocratic and very profligate gamblers. The lovely Georgian house had been burned down...across the road was the mausoleum which he describes in the poem...the sarcophagi had been robbed, the lead had been taken, naturally, and sheep used it as a refuge. After that we did swim, halfway up Galway harbor."

Despite her earlier enthusiasm for Ireland, it is not clear that Penelope, who was a teetotaller, enjoyed her three years in Dublin as a diplomat's wife. In particular she didn't like the Irish parties which started after dinner and involved drinking until the early hours, and it may be that it was at Penelope's behest that they left Dublin in 1943. On their parting visit to de Valera, Penelope said to him: "My husband knows nothing of politics; or of journalism. He knows nothing at all".

Which brings us to the third love which brought Betjeman from time to time to Ireland, and which was to cause heartache to both John and Penelope; Lady Elizabeth Cavendish. Betjeman met

Elizabeth at a dinner party given by Lady Pamela Berry, wife of the newspaper magnate, in 1951 when he was 46 and Elizabeth was a tall, shy young woman of 20. They said many years later that they had fallen in love over dinner and soon afterwards, on the Berry's' yacht on a cruise to Copenhagen, began an affair which was to last, as we saw earlier, until John Betjeman's death.

At first Penelope treated this like any other of his affairs "John was always falling in love" but Elizabeth, daughter of the tenth Duke of Devonshire was not interested in a casual affair. She was in love with him and over the years took on the role of his protectress. Early in their relationship he had nicknamed her "Feeble" or "Phoeble" in contrast to the more robust character of "Penelope" or "Philth". John Betjeman later settled on "Plymmi" for his wife; Plymouth more or less marks the boundary between Cornwall and the rest of England.

Opinion is divided as to whether Elizabeth was charming or not but she certainly possessed aristocratic sang-froid. In 1943, Kathleen "Kick" Kennedy (sister of the future President) wrote to her father about a London party:

"Lord Edward Fitzmaurice, a young guardsman of 21, had rather too much to drink and set a match to Lady Elizabeth Cavendish's new evening dress... [she] told her mother 'before I was set on fire the boys didn't pay much attention to me but afterwards I was very popular. An American boy put the flames out.'"

Kick Kennedy, of course, went on to marry the eldest son of the Duke of Devonshire, the Marquess of Hartington (who was at the same party) despite her parents' disapproval. He was killed in the war in Belgium, while she died in 1948 in a plane crash on the Riviera.

Both Elizabeth and John were devout and observant high church Anglicans, often attending Matins or Evensong together. Their relationship hurt Penelope deeply, so much so that she offered him a divorce, despite it being against her religious principles, and it hurt Elizabeth who had wanted a normal life of marriage and children. Betjeman feared that hell fire awaited him (and several of his poems are about his fear of death) because of the pain he caused to both the most important women in his life; but he couldn't give up either woman and, as it turned out, neither could give up John. Unlike Penelope, Elizabeth enjoyed a drink and was interested in literature and the arts.

In 1954, Elizabeth did try to end her affair with John Betjeman, for the sake of his marriage, but without success; they were too attached to each other. The poem this hiatus gestated, "The Cockney Amorist", has a striking similarity in sentiment to the poem he wrote on Penelope's conversion, quoted above:

> Oh when my love, my darling,
> You've left me here alone,
> I'll walk the street of London
> Which once seemed all our own.
>
> The vast suburban churches
> Together we have found:
> The ones which smelt of gaslight
> The ones in incense drown'd;
> I'll use them now for praying in
> And not for looking round....
>
> I love you, oh my darling,
> And what I can't make out
> Is why since you have left me
> I'm somehow still about.

Which might suggest to the cynic that the poetic tropes of love, abandonment and loss remain much the same whether the woman in question was the wife Penelope or the *maîtresse en titre* Elizabeth.

One of the Devonshire family houses is Lismore Castle in Co. Waterford and on several occasions after the war, they went to stay together at Lismore, forming another bond between John Betjeman and Ireland.

No doubt, Betjeman wrote many letters to Elizabeth but we will not see these until 2034 as she decided that all his letters to her should be kept in the Chatsworth archives for fifty years after his death. John Betjeman wrote to his great friend George Barnes (the "Commander") in 1951 that: "My new friend Elizabeth Cavendish is just our kind of girl. She is bracing and witty and kind and keen on drink as Anne. I long for you to meet her". Evidently more of a kindred spirit than Penelope, whom he loved despite their differences.

In 1974, Betjeman wrote to Billa Harrod, who had some personal experience of affairs, having spent most of her married life in love with another Oxford don, at length about Penelope and Elizabeth, the two greatest loves of his life:

"Darling Billa.... Your kindest action to me in our long and loving friendship was to speak to me so kindly and clearly of Penelope. I love her. But I cannot live with her for long without quarrelling. I sensed her anguish when we went to the cinema last night with Emily [Villiers-Stuart]. I cannot bear to hurt her... I have lived so long apart from Penelope that Elizabeth now loves me more than anyone else in the world. I cannot hurt *her* either...in all this awful storm of misery, the one thing I cling to is my love for Penelope *and* Elizabeth."

Lady Elizabeth Cavendish
(LUCIAN FREUD)

While Elizabeth did not much like Penelope, the complicated ménage à trois was to endure until his death. In 1955, while John Betjeman was on a tour of Bavaria, Austria and Venice with his mistress and members of her family, he wrote a letter to "My darling Plymmi [Penelope]" he concludes this letter with a poem which hints at the complexity of his feelings for Elizabeth, which must have made painful reading for his wife:

> Among the loud Americans
> *Zwei Engländer* were we,
> You so white and frail and pale
> And me so deeply me....
> In the Public Gardens,
> Ended things begin:
> *Ausgang* we were out of love
> *Und eingang* we are in

Of course, this might come across to the reader as self-pity or a case of both wanting to have one's cake and eat two of them, but the evidence is that Betjeman genuinely loved and cared for both women.

Ian Sansom, reviewing volume two of Bevis Hillier's biography of Betjeman for the *London Review of Books*, wrote: "Hillier, it should be noted, is defiantly pro-Betjeman, and perhaps just a little anti-Penelope, describing her at one point as 'horse-mad and cantankerous', which is a bit rich, since one might just as easily describe Betjeman as a silly little man with a taste for posh totty."

Betjeman continued to insist on his love for Penelope even when he had become the constant companion of Elizabeth Cavendish. In 1957, he writes to his wife: "Darling Plymmi, I have been thinking that probably why I love you more than anyone else in the world is because we are married in eternity and really cash, sex, kiddiz, good and bad fortune, fame and failure are all of less importance". Disavowing in the first two categories two of the principal drivers of his life, makes one wonder whether he was really trying to convince himself. Three months later, he and Penelope went to live for a few months in Cincinnati where John Betjeman had been given a temporary appointment to give a series of lectures on poetry.

He charmed many women because he possessed that most seductive of traits, the ability to make women laugh.

In his entertaining biography of Betjeman, A. N. Wilson opined that the English upper classes were happy to accommodate adultery but were much less inclined to look benignly on divorce, echoing the words of Billa Harrod. This was in contrast to the middle classes who were diametrically opposite, condemnatory of affairs and insistent that these could only be remedied by divorce. In this regard at least, John Betjeman effortlessly achieved the transition from one social class to another.

ON THE SLOW TRAIN

Most countries suffer certain privations in war time; neutral Ireland was no exception. Most fuel had to be imported from the UK, particularly coal and gasoline. Petrol rationing was draconian and the extensive rail network suffered from the dearth of coal, only occasionally available from the tenders of trains from Belfast when they reached Amiens Street station in Dublin.

But there was a substitute; turf. Ireland had vast quantities of this but it was a poor quality fuel of low calorific value; boiling a kettle over turf was as lengthy as the tiny gas flame allowed in towns and officiously policed by the "glimmer man". For trains, turf became the main fuel but prodigious quantities of ash meant the train had to be stopped every few miles while the fire basket was bailed out. On one memorable occasion a train from Killarney to Dublin, a journey now taking just over three hours, took twenty three hours.

Life slowed down. The fortunate few had limited rations of petrol, trains were uncertain, municipal trams in Dublin eventually stopped running and the country returned to the horse and cart. The mail boats continued to cross the Irish Sea but the journey time doubled and there was always the danger of attack. War planes were active in the area; there were several mistaken attacks by the Luftwaffe on Ireland and at least one by the RAF, despite the fact that the cities were lit up in contrast to the black-out throughout the UK.

Perhaps the lights shone less brightly; Ireland was fortunate to have the Shannon hydro-electric scheme but this could supply only a portion of the national consumption of electricity, the balance coming from turf burning power generators whose inefficiency meant that electricity was effectively rationed by frequent power cuts.

Not only was there the danger of mistaken air raids, there were frequent stories in the English Press of German U-Boats using facilities on the West coast of Ireland. Undoubtedly the IRA were involved in the supply of arms from Germany, but it is hard to imagine what the coastal dwellers of Connaught could offer to a U-Boat crew except for a few potatoes.

Potatoes, dairy products and meat were in plentiful supply and continued to be exported to the UK throughout the war; other foodstuffs such as fruit which required a warmer climate, pasta, flour were either very limited or non existent. Only those fortunate enough to have a cellar were able to enjoy this wine but whiskey and porter needed only home grown barley. A curious sweet drink called Irish sherry, which had no connection with the vineyards of Jerez de la Frontera, became ubiquitous. I came across its lineal descendant as a student fifty years ago in Dublin, a brand called Suvleen, described on the back label as "an exquisitely sweet chemical Irish wine".

Newsprint was also in short supply, although news was in any case rationed by strict censorship. No mention was to be made of victories or defeats on either side and, since none of the Irish newspapers had a foreign correspondent, their reporting abilities were limited. UK papers, which had a wide readership in Ireland, were subject to the same censorship.

At one point, when the chief censor was on holiday, his deputy banned mention of the word "war", rather like Vladimir Putin's "special operations" in the Ukraine. Ownership of wireless sets was widespread and, apart from tuning into Athlone, listeners could hear the Irish language broadcasts of the Irland Redaktion service from Nazi Germany or the BBC. But there was a problem, the batteries required re-charging or replacement and after two years of war this became very difficult.

Later in the war, both the US government led by Roosevelt and Churchill's government in London tried to persuade the Irish censors to be less impartial but they had only limited success.

Until the war, most Irish authors had published in the UK or the US, and a few in Paris, but this of course became difficult. The literary scene thrived in wartime Dublin, described in the section "The Palace Bar" and created a market for Irish based publishers, particularly the Talbot Press which had a list of more than 500 titles.

All of this added to the complexities of relationships between Ireland and Britain. This was the country in which Betjeman took up residence in the middle of the Second World War.

UNDERCOVER IN DUBLIN

By 1940, Europe was in darkness. Hitler's Wehrmacht had swept across the continent, France had fallen and only the British Empire still battled against the Nazi tide. There were still a few pools of light in the blackout: Sweden, Switzerland, Spain and Ireland; these remained neutral in a Nazi occupied Europe from Russia to the French Atlantic coast. All four of these countries were convinced that the UK would be defeated within a year; Sweden had allowed Germany to build a railway to facilitate its invasion of Norway, Switzerland had a German speaking majority, Franco in Spain had recently been aided by the German Condor Legion to win the civil war, and there were some in Ireland, still with bitter memories of the Troubles before and after independence, who perhaps looked forward to the prospect of the defeat of Britain.

However, Irish neutrality was a great deal more nuanced than is suggested by those who only mention De Valera signing the book of condolences at the German Embassy to Dublin on Hitler's suicide. Not only did many thousands of Irish people join the Allied war effort, Ireland was a vital source of food imports for Britain throughout the war; Allied flyers whose planes had come down in Ireland found their route to the border with the North facilitated. Officers of the Royal Navy were welcome visitors at both Cork harbour and on the Shannon estuary where they supervised the installation of heavy defence guns. Shells for these guns were secretly supplied to the Irish government in nighttime convoys from Northern Ireland. Crucially, of course, the famous weather forecast which averted a D-Day catastrophe, was telephoned through from Blacksod Bay in Co. Mayo.

Combatants from both sides interned in the Curragh were allowed out at weekends to go to race meetings but only Allied internees were given money to bet on the horses, while Allied officers were granted parole to attend parties in Dublin; detention was not onerous compared to Stalag Luft VII.

There is some evidence that the Ministry of Information under Brendan Bracken (who was very close to Churchill) deliberately fostered the idea that Ireland was pro German in order to protect Ireland's neutral status.

Ireland had been a sovereign nation for less than twenty years and sentiment between the UK and Ireland was, at times, less than cordial. The UK government had withdrawn from the Boundary Commission in 1924, regarded in Ireland as a hostile act.

We also tend to forget that Partition, such a bitter bone of contention, was opposed before independence by most of the Westminster establishment and was only acceded to because of the potent threats of Carson, leader of the Unionists. My grandfather, Richard Preston, writing from his office in London to his brother Lord Gormanston, says that he now thinks Sinn Fein less of a danger than Edward Carson and in colourful language (and difficult handwriting) appears to go on to say that he'd "sooner be b…ered by a hen than be in a railway carriage with Carson".

De Valera, leader of the anti-treaty party Fianna Fáil, had achieved power in the 1937 election. In particular there was resentment in England at the loss of the three treaty ports. Winston Churchill (a back bench MP at the time) had addressed the House of Commons on this issue in 1938 and his words (which I quote at some length because they provide a useful context) are representative of the tone of the British Press:

"When I read this Agreement in the newspapers a week ago I was filled with surprise. On the face of it, we seem to give everything away and receive nothing in return...But then I supposed there was another side to the Agreement, and that we were to be granted some facilities and rights in Southern Ireland in time of war. That, I notice, was the view taken by a part of the Press, but soon Mr. de Valera in the Dáil made it clear that he was under no obligations of any kind and, as the Prime Minister confirmed ...On the contrary, Mr. de Valera has not even abandoned his claim for the incorporation of Ulster...

We are told that we have ended the age-long quarrel between England and Ireland, but that is clearly not true, because Mr. de Valera has said that he will never rest until Partition is swept away. Therefore, the real conflict has yet to come...[The Anglo-Irish] Treaty has been kept in the letter and the spirit by Great Britain, but the Treaty has been violated and repudiated in every detail by Mr. de Valera. The ports in question, Queenstown, Berehaven and Lough Swilly, are to be handed over unconditionally, with no guarantees of any kind, as a gesture of our trust and goodwill, as the Prime Minister said, to the Government of the Irish Republic.

When the Irish Treaty was being shaped in 1922 I was instructed

Éamon de Valera
(NATIONAL PHOTO COMPANY COLLECTION – LIBRARY OF CONGRESS)

by the Cabinet to prepare that part of the Agreement which dealt with strategic reservations. I negotiated with Mr. Michael Collins, and I was advised by Admiral Beatty. The Admiralty of those days assured me that without the use of these ports it would be very difficult, perhaps almost impossible, to feed this Island in time of war. Queenstown and Berehaven…are, in fact, the sentinel towers of the western approaches, by which the 45,000,000 people in this Island so enormously depend on foreign food for their daily bread, and by which they can carry on their trade, which is equally important to their existence.

In 1922 the Irish delegates made no difficulty about this. They saw that it was vital to our safety that we should be able to use these ports and, therefore, the matter passed into the structure of the Treaty without any serious controversy. Now we are to give them up, unconditionally, to an Irish Government led by men [about whom] I do not want to use hard words whose rise to power has been proportionate to the animosity with which they have acted against this country, no doubt in pursuance of their own patriotic impulses, and whose present position in power is based upon the violation of solemn Treaty engagements.

But what guarantee have you that Southern Ireland, or the Irish Republic, as they claim to be and you do not contradict them will not declare neutrality if we are engaged in war with some powerful nation? Under this Agreement, it seems to me...that Mr. de Valera's Government will at some supreme moment of emergency demand the surrender of Ulster as an alternative to declaring neutrality.

Mr. de Valera has given no undertaking, except to fight against Partition as the main object of his life. It would be a serious step for a Dublin Government to attack these ports while they are in our possession and while we have the right to occupy them. It would be an easy step for a Dublin Government to deny their use to us once we have gone... You are casting away real and important means of security and survival for vain shadows and for ease."

This continued to rankle; more than sixty years after the end of the war, *The Times* published a letter which read as follows:

"Sir, John Betjeman may have considered Mr. de Valera 'Britain's best friend in Ireland' (letter, Aug 23) but the Taoiseach proved that he was certainly no friend of the UK during the Second World War. His refusal to allow the southern Treaty Ports (foolishly surrendered by Chamberlain before the war) to be used by British naval craft to further their range against U-boat attacks on the North Atlantic convoys not only caused greater loss of needed supplies and lives of British seamen but was breath-taking in its hypocrisy as Ireland still received from Britain its quota of food imports from the hard-pressed convoys."

Such was the importance of these ports to the war effort that there is evidence that Churchill considered bargaining Northern Ireland's place within the UK in return for their use.

The IRA had resumed attacks on the UK in 1939-40; on 16 January 1939 bombs were planted in Southwark, Willesden, Birmingham, Manchester, and Alnwick which unsurprisingly increased anti Irish feeling.

Although some members of the Irish government were ambivalent about the prospect of the eagerly anticipated Hitler's defeat of Britain, de Valera was more prescient in foreseeing that a total Nazi triumph might herald the end of democracy. Moreover, he had a good reason for demanding the return of the Treaty Ports; had they continued as bases for the Royal Navy this would have compromised the neutrality of Ireland and offered a clear *casus belli* to Germany.

International law demanded that any nation which claimed territorial waters must have an armed presence within them. With due solemnity, an officer in the Irish army, armed with a revolver, was rowed by a soldier in a small boat down the River Liffey into Dublin Bay and the nation's naval presence was thus asserted.

The anti-Irish sentiment in the British Press was reciprocated in Ireland, not by the *Irish Times* which still remained the journal of the vanishing Anglo-Irish Ascendancy but in other outlets, and it was studiously fomented by the German Embassy in Dublin.

Memories of the times of extreme poverty, of the Penal Laws, the workhouses, tyrannical English landlords and famine were still fresh. Independence had only recently been won and anti-British sentiment was understandably present.

The Anglo-Irish themselves were part of the divide; their primary loyalty was to the Crown and not to the Free State. They volunteered in large numbers to join the British forces, but so did thousands of ordinary Irishmen who felt that Hitler should be resisted. It has recently been estimated that 50,000 Irish men and women joined the British armed forces or worked in some way for the Allied war effort.

Ireland was still a member of the Commonwealth but had never agreed to the Dominion status of countries such as Canada and Australia; so the UK could not have an Embassy nor a High Commission in Dublin, instead they decided on a Mission which was headed by a retired diplomat, Sir John Maffey (later Lord Rugby). He summed up his views of Ireland at the end of the war as follows:

"Today, after six years detachment, Eire is more than ever a foreign country...so dominated by the National Catholic Church as to be almost a theocratic state…anti-British feeling is fostered in school and by Church and State by a system of hereditary enemy indoctrination." Sir John Maffey in a 1945 Memorandum to the Secretary of State for the Dominions.

Maffey had had a distinguished career in India and the Sudan, culminating in his appointment in the Civil Service as Permanent

Under-Secretary of State for the Colonies. He was persuaded to come out of retirement by Neville Chamberlain to negotiate and then lead the British Mission to Eire, where he successfully mediated between the stridently opposing views of de Valera and Winston Churchill, later also establishing cordial relationships with the Costello government.

The family connection was to be maintained; in 1962 Maffey's grand daughter, Maria Aitken (later famous as an actress) prevailed upon Betjeman to give a talk to the sixth form at her school, Sherborne. She clearly knew how to persuade Betjeman writing that "Miss Reader-Harris, who is, incidentally, the most beautiful headmistress in England, would give you an excellent dinner and put you up for the night".

Maffey's daughter, Penelope, later Lady Aitken had written to her father about the arrival of the Betjemans in Ireland: "I think he should be very good. The couple have a big reputation here, both rather eccentric and intellectual . . . he should be the sort of whimsical person the Irish like, and he likes them." Much later Betjeman told Penelope Maffey that when she came into the room, he went weak at the knees. She was described in her obituary in *The Times* as exuding warmth and sex appeal.

Clearly, this was a troubled atmosphere thick with mutual suspicion, distrust and dislike but also strong connections of family, history and economic interest into which heady and complicated mix arrived Betjeman, a poet not a diplomat, in 1941. His task at the British Mission was to improve the sentiment in media coverage on both sides of the Irish Sea. He was an inspired choice, principally because, as we have seen, John Betjeman had fallen in love with Ireland on first acquaintance, 16 years before his posting to Dublin.

Sir John Maffey, later Lord Rugby
(PHOTOGRAPHER UNKNOWN – NATIONAL PORTRAIT GALLERY, LONDON)

Despite this affection, Betjeman was not happy in the early days with his job in Dublin. Writing in 1941, just after he had returned from Holyhead where he had fetched Penelope and their son Paul, to his habitual confidants, the Pipers, he observed:

"I wish I cared more about the war, then I would care more about my job. All able-bodied pro-British have left Ireland for the English services and we are at the mercy of people who are either anti-British... The Irish papers are all anti-British and the best-selling writers are pro-German. I am beginning to hate Ireland and the Irish." And to Kenneth Clark a few months later: "I am devoted to Maffey but many more months here being jolly with second-raters will anyhow send me off my head."

English newspapers circulated freely in Ireland, although supply was constrained by lack of newsprint, transport and occasional bans by the Irish censor if they contained information which was blatantly anti-Irish. In fact, the *Daily Mail* increased its share of the Irish market during the war. A major part of Betjeman's task was to ameliorate the anti-Irish tone of the British Press.

Halfway through his Dublin posting, John Betjeman was to write to the publisher Hamish Hamilton urging him to send review copies to the *Irish Press* ("the government paper here, whose editor M. J. MacManus is a great friend of mine") and to the *Irish Independent*. John Betjeman was equally keen to dilute the anti-English tone of much of the Press in Ireland, apart from the *Irish Times*.

John Betjeman believed, in contrast to Churchill, that, if the six counties of Northern Ireland were ceded to the Irish state, that might induce de Valera to abandon neutrality and join the Allied cause. There is no evidence to support his views and Churchill was more worried about the deep-water harbours of

Londonderry and Belfast Lough which were vital naval bases for protecting the Atlantic convoys, on which Britain's survival depended. Indeed, Churchill was more concerned that Nazi Germany would invade Ireland as a stepping stone to invading the UK mainland. The defeat of the Luftwaffe in the Battle of Britain in 1940 and the subsequent defeat of the German navy in the Battle of the Atlantic in 1941 made the latter possibility remote but Ireland continued to be an attempted base for German espionage although this was laughable in its inefficiency.

By the time the USA belatedly entered the war in 1942 when, post Pearl Harbour, Adolf Hitler, possibly unwisely, declared war on the US, the issue of Ireland as a potential bridgehead for a Nazi invasion was no longer salient. Churchill had been busy trying to persuade the USA to enter the war; Joe Kennedy (father of JFK) the US Ambassador to London had been equally busy opposing this, predicting the swift fall of Britain. In the end Hitler made the decision. As a later politician was to remark, most political outcomes are decided by "events, dear boy, events".

While the Galway man (although born in the USA), William Joyce (Lord Haw Haw) broadcast Nazi propaganda in English, the German propaganda ministry under Goebbels, also had a dedicated unit which broadcast in Gaelic aimed at Ireland. Originally based in Berlin, the Irland-Redaktion service broadcast throughout the war, being moved towards the fall of the Third Reich to Luxembourg to avoid Allied bombers. Whether it had a significant listenership in Ireland is unknown but it was used to send coded messages to German agents in Ireland who collaborated with the IRA in offensives against the UK. Its history is detailed in David O'Donoghue's scholarly work, *Hitler's Irish Voices*.

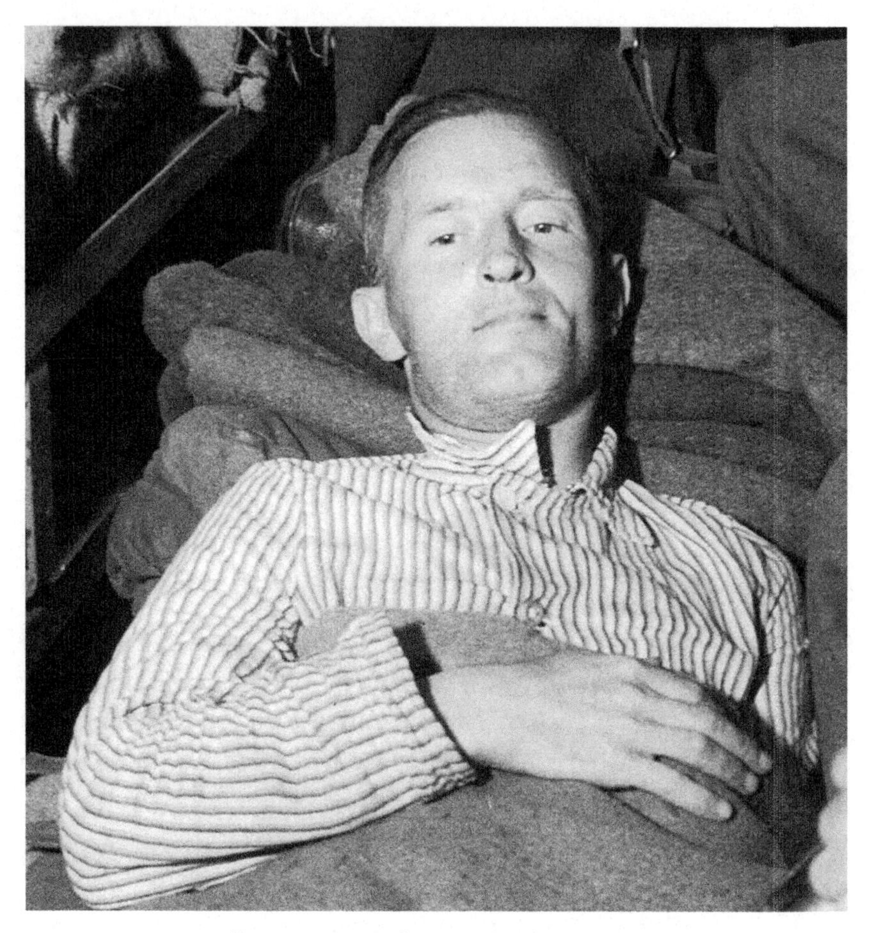

William Joyce, Lord Haw Haw (BERT HARDY)

Betjeman had stepped into a metaphorical minefield with little resource except his natural affability.

In 1938 John Betjeman had enlisted in the Observer Corps, the group responsible for tracking the movement of aircraft over the UK. After war broke out, despite some pacifist doubts, he tried to enlist in the RAF but was rejected on medical grounds. He later joked that this was because he had disclosed his fear of spiders although it is doubtful if arachnophobia would alone have prevented him from flying aircraft. Rejected next by the Royal Marines, he tried to enlist the efforts of the Field Marshal, his father-in-law, who seems to have been equally dubious as to John Betjeman's martial abilities as he had earlier been about his marital suitability. What Chetwode did do was to urge Betjeman to take a job in the Ministry of Information with Sir Kenneth Clark (later to win renown for his "Civilisation" series for the BBC). At the time Clark was a very young and recently knighted Director of the National Gallery in Trafalgar Square.

As the blitz raged, Clark's first task was to protect the picture collection of the National Gallery which was sent for storage in a disused Welsh slate mine. He went on to arrange lunchtime and early evening concerts at the Gallery throughout the war, cheering the spirits of many civilians and military. In the era of "snowflakes" we sometimes forget that throughout the blitz, theatres, churches, restaurants and pubs remained open.

John Betjeman had first met Clark at Oxford with Maurice Bowra; Clark valued his originality and creativity. In January 1941, it was at his recommendation, that John Betjeman was appointed Press Attaché to the British Mission in Dublin.

Penelope was not keen, at this stage, on moving to Ireland or of moving anywhere. John Betjeman wrote to his old friend Gerard Irvine saying he too was loth to move, although he signed himself Seán O'Betjemán.

Betjeman's mother was worried that "the Huns (might) invade Ireland". The family arrived (John as the advance party) with their infant son, Paul and Betty the nanny, lodging first as paying guests in a house near the Phoenix Park owned by two spinsters, the Misses Hamilton, who were, according to Betjeman, terrible artists. Poor artists they may have been but their connections with the worlds of artists and aristocrats in Ireland were to prove helpful to Betjeman in the six months he and his family lived there.

Dunsinea House was so damp that mould grew on Betjeman's black suits in days but Penelope was cheered by the arrival of her horse, Moti, from England. Moti had been a present from her father when she was in India and was painted by Lord Berners.

Gerald Berners, was a rich aesthete who lived at Faringdon close to the Betjemans. A great friendship developed which was to last until his death in 1950. He insisted on painting Penelope astride Moti in his drawing room. Her concern that horse dung would not enhance the Aubusson carpets was dismissed with lordly insouciance; what else are servants for he asked. Lord Berners is now better remembered as the model for Lord Merlin in Nancy Mitford's novel, *The Pursuit of Love*.

Back to Dunsinea: a chance meeting at a party with Major Billy Kirkwood and his wife Peta, a member of the Jameson whiskey dynasty, led to the offer of Collinstown House in the fields and winding farm lanes of Clondalkin, at a token rent and complete with eleven polo ponies, which suited Penelope very well. The house was crumbling and damp, there was no electricity, the area not attractive, most goods were in very short supply, especially petrol, wine, fruits but the Betjeman family settled in there. With the house came Maeve the maid, one of whose duties was to sprinkle holy water each morning on the Press Attaché's car to ensure that it would start. Despite its drawbacks, photographs show it as an elegant Georgian house; it has since been demolished.

Betjeman had his office at the Mount St Mission painted "boudoir pink" and decorated it with etchings by his great friend John Piper showing London churches damaged in the blitz.

Betjeman's opposite number at the German Dublin Embassy was Karl Petersen (nearly the same name as the arch villain in Sapper's Bulldog Drummond novels) who, when sober, effectively propagandised for the Nazi government. More concerning to the British was that the German Minister in Dublin, Eduard Hempel, had established cordial relations with de Valera, the Irish leader and of course Hempel adroitly exploited the mutual dislike between de Valera and Winston Churchill.

In a letter to John Piper from Collinstown House dated the first Sunday after the Epiphany 1941, Betjeman writes: "Hallo is that John Betjemann? Oi'v just heard that England's had a licken. 'Who told you?' Karl. 'Did you read moi review naow?' I did. Was it the one in the *Irish Times*?' 'It was not, it was in the *Capuchin Annual*'.... And here reviews, libels, back-chat, high tea, cold, no petrol, no light, no coal, no trains...propaganda, propaganda, propaganda."

Betjeman was a success. His natural charm, enthusiasm and affability transcended many historic antipathies. He even impressed Frank Gallagher, the sceptical Director of the Irish Government Information Service. When he declared his intention to learn Gaelic, Gallaher, who put him in touch with a teacher, thought he would soon be bored; but John Betjeman loved it; he would practice phrases aloud on the top deck of the bus going from Clondalkin to the Mission in Mount Street and within a couple of years became fluent enough to write entire letters in Gaelic. His daughter, Candida, recounts that he taught her brother Paul to count in Gaelic before he could do so in English.

A mutual friend of the Pakenhams, F. MacNeice Foster, wrote to Betjeman in 1941: "He (Frank Pakenham) formed the impression quite clearly that in a short time you had carved out a niche for yourself in a way which no other Englishman had done, and had won the confidence of a number of extremists who normally were quite proof against British blandishments. He was, quite seriously, immensely impressed."

Among the people who became friends were Sean MacEntee, a government minister, and his wife. MacEntee, with a background of fighting in the 1916 uprising had little reason for affection for the English but as one of his daughters, Máire (later the second wife of Conor Cruise O'Brien and herself a poet in both English and Irish) wrote: "Both my parents absolutely loved the Betjemans… I think the Betjemans loved them too". There were several memorable parties at the home of the MacEntees as there were at the house of Erskine Childers (son of the novelist shot by Michael Collins' side in 1922). One of the latter parties involved John Betjeman and Childers in the small hours of the morning trying to cover up a huge swastika which had been dug on the lawn by the very drunk Francis MacNamara, father in law of the poet and often equally drunk, Dylan Thomas.

Máire MacEntee, as she then was, recounted how she was taught as a child that on visits to Austria and Germany, should anyone greet her with Heil Hitler, she was to reply: *Dia's Muire dhuit* in Irish meaning "God and Mary be with you". So are diplomats trained from an early age.

Betjeman was less successful in winning over Archbishop McQuaid, the austere prelate who ruled the Catholic Church with an iron fist and had a strong influence over successive governments. John Betjeman recognised the immense power of the church in Ireland but McQuaid was not to be won over by charm and in particular was angered when a member of the Polish Government in exile, Count Balinski, visiting Dublin at Betjeman's invitation, dared to criticise the Irish censor. McQuaid was posthumously vilified for managing the practise of selling babies for adoption, forcibly removed from their mothers, to couples in America.

As we shall see in the next chapter (see p. 97), there was also a much more human side to Archbishop McQuaid. Betjeman had rather more success in becoming on friendly terms with Cardinal McRory, the Primate of all Ireland, possibly because they shared similar views on the partition of Ireland.

The only notable religious triumph Betjeman pulled off in his time in Ireland was when he had arranged for Laurence Olivier to come to Ireland for the filming of Shakespeare's *Henry V*. On Sunday he insisted that they should all attend High Mass at Maynooth, fully aware of what the gratifying headlines on Monday would read.

Henry V was an obvious choice for a Shakespeare film in the middle of the war as, of course, it celebrates the glorious victory of the English at Agincourt and is chiefly remembered for the rousing, patriotic St Crispin's Day speech which ends with the exhortation by the King to his troops before the battle:

> We few, we happy few, we band of brothers;
> For he to-day that sheds his blood with me
> Shall be my brother; be he ne'er so vile,
> This day shall gentle his condition;
> And gentlemen in England now a-bed
> Shall think themselves accurs'd they were not here,
> And hold their manhoods cheap whiles any speaks
> That fought with us upon Saint Crispin's day

Sir Laurence Olivier (ALLEN WARREN)

Ironically, the English infantry in the film, requiring a good many actors, was supplied by the Irish army.

Filmed at Powerscourt House in Co. Wicklow, this was Laurence Olivier's debut as a director. Ireland was chosen partly because the skies of England were filled with battling warplanes in 1943. Powerscourt was picked because John Betjeman, who was instrumental in using the filming for positive propaganda, had brought Olivier and Dallas Bower (whom John Betjeman had first met in 1934 when he was with one of his amours, Nerina Shute) to lunch with Edward Longford who said to the two directors "The man for you is Mervyn Powerscourt".

The filming did not go without several hitches. The cavalry, or at least their mounts, caught a bug and Lord Powerscourt ordered them off his estate for fear they should infect his horses. Olivier and Bowers found the damp of Collinstown House, where the Betjemans lived in Clondalkin, unbearable and decamped to the slightly greater comfort of the Shelbourne Hotel, but the film was successfully finished.

Betjeman wrote to Jane, wife of Sir Kenneth Clark in June 1943: "Dear Jane, Thank you so much for having me to stay the other night in that quiet luxury. The Journey back was interrupted for me – I had some W. B. Maxwell novels to read which I hadn't read – by the presence of L [Olivier] and old Dallas Bower who was on the train bound for Eire to direct *Henry V* at Powerscourt. That nice lesbian-looking chauffeuse you secured for me was very pleased to see Olivier at Euston and shouted out, 'Hi-di-ho! Larry! My brother was at school with you'. There was a very attractive secretary with L Olivier, who had been in the tennis team of Malvern Girls College.".

Powerscourt House, County Wicklow (AMANDA SUSAN MUNROE)

Not surprisingly, most of the good friends Betjeman made in this period in Dublin were part of the world of arts and letters, covered in the next section. It was with these people, very different from the members of the Anglo-Irish Ascendancy who had hitherto formed his Irish acquaintance, that he was happiest while in Dublin for nearly three years.

Thirty years after the war had ended he was still sympathetic to the difficulties partition had created in Ireland, offering his support to a letter urging that the stationing of British troops in Northern Ireland be time limited, provided that the authors first consulted George Simms, the Archbishop of Armagh whom Betjeman clearly thought of as a wise man.

He mocked his political difficulties; in another letter to John Piper and his wife Myfanwy (the latter the subject of some of Betjeman's best erotic poetry) in 1941, he wrote:

"Dear Mr Papher, darling Goldilox,
I am writing this on the GNR (Great Northern Railway) in a flash cocktail bar on the train. Propellor [one of his names for Penelope] and I have been staying on the border. It is perfectly easy to cross it with no interference...I am afraid I often think of Goldilox's figure, hair and face and it compares very favourably with all colleens.

Martin Travers' [an architect] daughter Sally, who acts over here with a repertory company is pro-German and sleeps with my opposite number. He is so unpopular here except among politically minded tarts and stockbroking and layer place-hunters that he does his cause more harm than good. I am a little sunbeam and very pure in contrast...

Is mise le meas mor, Seán O'B"

Many years after the war, the accusation was made that John Betjeman had been a spy while at the British Mission. In so far as part of the job of any diplomat is to pass intelligence back to his own government, he may have been but he was unlikely to have been a spy in any active sense.

Ironically, his Germanic surname had been the occasion when he was a small boy in the First World War of the taunt: "Betjeman's a German spy/Shoot him down and let him die" wrote John Betjeman in his verse autobiography *Summoned by Bells,* referring to his childhood persecutors at Highgate School.

The IRA were sufficiently convinced to hatch a plot to assassinate Betjeman. Diarmuid Brennan wrote to Betjeman twenty-two years after the war had ended explaining that the Army Council of the IRA had decided that he was a "person of menace" and should be murdered although the plan was later abandoned as the would-be assassins were under Garda surveillance. A more amusing but untrue version suggested the plot was abandoned because a senior IRA figure read and enjoyed the poet's verses. Diplomatic immunity was, and remained, no guarantee of safety in Dublin if the embassy in question was that of the United Kingdom. In 1976, only a few weeks after his arrival as Ambassador to Dublin, the IRA murdered Christopher Ewart-Biggs.

Betjeman was more light hearted about the accusation that he was a spy. In March 1941, he wrote to Frank O'Connor (the pseudonym of Michael O'Donovan, a writer and journalist with a fine West Cork baritone):

"Dear Poet,
Delighted to hear from old Seán O'Faoláin that you are back. Look at me, a bloody British spy (open) Press Attaché here. Now you can both come in to Dublin for lunch…the O'Faoláins are coming…

Did I tell you that Lord Wicklow was once taken to the opera in London to hear Wagner. He fell asleep and his hostess said to him, 'How do you like it?' He woke up and replied, 'Sounds to me like Willesden Junction.'"

But clearly spying was afoot in neutral Dublin. In the same year on St Patrick's Day, he writes to John Piper: "A woman who is pro-Nazi and thinks she is a spy has made a pass at me and I have been through embarrassing scenes in motor cars."

Betjeman's primary asset was his ability to engage people in conversation and make friends. While he arranged for speakers

Seán O'Faoláin
(HOWARD COSTER, NATIONAL PORTRAIT GALLERY, LONDON)

to come to Ireland, not always with the blessing of the Dublin government, and initiated cultural events, it was through conversations that he had the greatest influence on relations between the two countries.

In this he was similar to Elizabeth Bowen, the novelist, who from her home of Bowen's Court in Co. Cork, sent regular reports to the Dominions Office in London on the temperature of opinion in Ireland with regard to the war, and was assiduous in trying to counter what she saw as anti-British propaganda.

There is some evidence that Betjeman was copied on the content of Elizabeth Bowen's reports to the government in London. Elizabeth Bowen remained at Bowen's Court until 1960, writing, entertaining, and occasionally having affairs with many prominent literary figures. Seán O'Faoláin was among her lovers.

Her family came to North Cork from Wales as part of the Cromwellian settlement, and Elizabeth inherited Bowen's Court on the death of her father, Henry, in 1930. She wrote many novels, several of them set in an Ascendancy Big House in North Cork, chronicling the declining years of the Anglo-Irish gentry.

Seán O'Faoláin was the editor of *The Bell* when John Betjeman was in Dublin and introduced him to Elizabeth Bowen. Shortage of money led her to sell her beloved house to a local man who promised to cherish it. He destroyed it a year later and she died in Hythe in Kent, in 1973 after a final Christmas visit to Kinsale, in a house she had named Carbery after the West Cork Barony. Betjeman and Bowen remained in touch; in 1964 he wrote to her asking for her to find help for an Irish writer, Norah Hoult, who had fallen on hard times.

Membership of the Cork Brigade of the IRA was no obstacle to

O'Faoláin winning a Commonwealth scholarship to study at Yale University. As editor of the most influential Irish literary magazine of the period, *The Bell*, anti-clerical but not anti-religious; with his friend the portly Capuchin, Fr Senan, he was to be seen attending every first night in the Dublin theatres. Fr Senan was also an acquaintance of John Betjeman's; he was the editor of a Catholic literary magazine, the *Capuchin Annual*, so lavishly produced that Fr Senan brought the Capuchin order close to bankruptcy. The order survives and the journal continued until 1977.

A measure of John Betjeman's success in his Dublin posting was not only the farewell party given for himself and Penelope by the MacEntees, at which Betjeman sang in fluent Irish, "Dark Rosaleen" – sixteen verses – with the tears pouring down his face (as Ruth Ellen Moller another daughter of the McEntees was to write later); but the fact that his departure was announced on the front page of the *Irish Times*; in a full length of page column, complete with photograph. The journalist wrote:

"He took the highest possible view of his duties as Press Attaché and looked upon it as his duty not only to interpret England to the Irish, but also to interpret Ireland sympathetically to the English, and if any English pressman or visitor went away with an unsympathetic view of Ireland it was not the fault of Mr Betjeman."

Nine decades after these events it is interesting to reflect that governments have always broken treaties when it suited them (whatever happened to the Molotov Ribbentrop pact?); that even in time of war there were no obstacles to crossing the Northern Irish border; that mutual prejudice and hostility are only broken down by human interactions. Betjeman brought charm and a deep affection for Ireland to try to mend some of the divisions between the two countries; the modern world continues to need such goodwill.

The Irish connection was not severed when the Betjemans returned to England. Posted to the old Admiralty building in Bath, Betjeman, it is rumoured, began an affair with Honor Tracy, a convert to the Church of Rome with a fondness for a drink or two. Her novels satirise Anglo-Irish relations and the Irish themselves with both comedy and bitterness. Honor links John Betjeman with the novelist Iris Murdoch as she slept with both of them. However, the rumour might only owe its existence to a spat between two biographers.

He also at the same time fell in love with Alice Hardy who had been assigned to him as his PE (BBC language for an assistant or Personal Executive), a term which made John Betjeman laugh uproariously.

Betjeman took very few things seriously, indeed one of his chief pleasures was comic invention; it is questionable whether he ever really took his job in Dublin seriously and perhaps this lightness of touch explains why he was such a success. His attitude is best summed up in a letter he wrote to Myfanwy Piper (Margaret Short was his secretary at the British Mission):

> United Kingdom Representative to Eire
> 50 Upper Mount Street, Dublin
> 3 May 1943
>
> Oh darling Goldilegz I often wish
> That you were Margaret Short. I seem to see
> Your strong blonde body curving through the reeds
> At Shiplake while I await you in the punt

And Mr Piper sketches in the fields
Oh darling Goldilegz I write this down
Dunsany-wise, straight off, so full of sex
That as I write even my fountain pen
Becomes symbolic to me. Goldilegz
Still do you sweep your short hair off your brow?
Still do you run barelegg'd across the yard?
Still would you pillow with athletic curves
My bald, grey head upon your breasts?
Your stalwart body still excites me much
The thought of you, now spring is coming on,
Requires that I should exercise control

And in the margins he wrote: "*Specially designed to shock the censor who has taken to reading our letters.*"

It was with mixed emotions that John Betjeman, with Penelope and his two children, Paul and Candida, prepared to leave Ireland; a sense of duty in returning to England but also happy memories of the friendships he had formed in his Dublin posting. By June 1943, it was clear to everyone, except the leaders of the Third Reich, and a handful of their more deluded sympathisers, that the defeat of Germany and the liberation of Europe was only a matter of time. He wrote to Frank Gallaher, Director of the GIS who was to make the speech at the leaving party at Dublin Castle for the Betjemans:

"We [he and his wife] both have responsibilities in England. First our village life where the Vicar (Anglo-Catholic) is old and ill and wants us to help with the church life of the village as we used to do; and second, the need to be in England during all the post-war reconstruction schemes... Living in Ireland has been a wonderful experience, because it is a wholly Christian country".

Gallaher concluded his farewell speech at Dublin Castle: "We shall remember them. One thing they will carry with them as proof of Irish hospitality is that they came three and went four... To the four of them we wish the Irish blessing *Dia go deo libh*."

The affection remained; in 1946 Frank Gallaher had asked John Betjeman to write a positive essay on Anglo-Irish relations and he had agreed. He wrote again to Gallaher:

"I am immensely grateful to you for your criticisms... The remarks of Insany's [Lord Dunsany]...I will expunge...the remarks about the nuncio should never have appeared... I hope the result will inform the thousands of English visitors you will be getting, of how to get on in Ireland, and how to appreciate the ancient nation Ireland is."

THE PALACE BAR

When John Betjeman began his posting to Dublin, he was, as we have seen, less than happy with being in Ireland despite his strong affection for the country. He felt that he should have been in England when it was at war and he was pessimistic about the possibility of achieving anything in his job; "The Irish papers are all anti-British and the best-selling writers are pro-German. I am beginning to hate Ireland and the Irish."

But by the time he was preparing to leave Dublin, nearly three years later, his opinion had changed completely. He wrote to Frank Gallaher in 1943:

"Dear Frank, Thank you so much for your kind letter. It all sounds rather like a bereavement and it is one. I am very depressed at going. So many friends made, so much kindness… might as well take this opportunity of thanking you for all the kindnesses you have done me…getting interviews with the Taoiseach – to whom I am greatly indebted and do convey my thanks to him – and for hospitality and gaiety in the past… Oh dear, I am sad. Yours, John B."

What had changed his feelings might be summed up under

the name of the Palace Bar. This was a pub in Fleet Street, Dublin which was not just the watering hole for the editor and journalists of the *Irish Times*, but of a miscellany of writers, poets and artists.

Hitherto, most of John Betjeman's Irish acquaintances had been members of the Anglo-Irish Ascendancy whom he had met while up at Oxford. Now he was to meet quite different members of Irish society.

R. M. Smyllie, editor of the *Irish Times*, held court in the Palace Bar. Attended by journalists, sycophants, those hoping to sell a story and those just hoping to cadge a drink, Smyllie had remade the *Irish Times*, journal of the Protestant Anglo-Irish, in his own fashion. He introduced humour and gently mocked the Dublin government.

Brian Inglis recalled him at the Island Golf Club: "Among the new members was a short, burly man who wore his disreputable clothes with an air of someone who has nothing better to wear—not, as other members did, because they kept shabby old clothes in the club house to change into. Robert Máire Smyllie was not, to look at, a man who could normally have expected to become a member of the Island, but it would have been difficult to exclude him; he was the editor of the *Irish Times*."

Bertie Smyllie was born in Glasgow seven years before the turn of the century and went up to Trinity College Dublin in 1912. He had the misfortune to take a vacation job as tutor to an American boy in Berlin during the First World War and was interned in Ruhleben camp outside Berlin. Returning to Dublin, he joined the *Irish Times* and succeeded John Healy as Editor in 1934. While the paper remained firmly the journal of the Ascendancy, by now very much in their twilight, Smyllie modernised it in several respects such as substituting Dun Laoghaire for Kingstown and Cobh for Queenstown; a dozen years after Irish independence this was probably wise.

Smyllie was a larger-than-life character, his fingers stained by printer's ink, like all the best of the old school of editors. Patrick Campbell (Lord Glenavy a Dublin born journalist and author), whom he recruited among others (including Lionel Fleming, to whom we will return later) as a columnist, wrote a charming memoir of Smyllie for the *Spectator* in 1959, which read in part:

"He was a classical scholar, at home among the Greek philosophers. He was the incorruptible champion of the fading Protestant cause in holy Ireland. His political and humanitarian views won international respect, and he spent most of his time on the run from the importunities of such characters as Chloral O'Kelly and Twitchy Doyle.

They lay in wait for him every evening in their chosen lairs in the front office and threw them-selves in his path, as though to halt a rushing loco-motive, as soon as he appeared at the door.

Chloral O'Kelly was a deeply melancholic youth who drank disinfectant, and was in constant need of 3s. 9d. for another bottle. Twitchy Doyle was a little old man with a straggly, jumping moustache who lived by reviewing reprints of Zane Grey. The moment the Editor burst through the front door they closed on him with urgent appeals, battling for position with Deirdre of the Sorrows, an elderly woman who believed for twelve years that she was being underpaid for her contributions to the Woman's Page. The Editor shot through them, weaving and jinking, crying: 'No – not tonight – tomorrow – goodbye'–

and put on an extra burst of speed which carried him up the stairs to the safety of his own room, there to deliver his unforgettable cry: 'Pismires! War-locks! Stand aside!'"

Among those who gathered in the circles around R. M. Smyllie were artists such as William Conor, Harry Kernoff, Jerome Connor, Seán O'Sullivan, Paul Henry, the playwright Brinsley MacNamara, the director of the Abbey Theatre Roibeard Ó Faracháin, and the actor Liam Redmond. Writers came regularly to the Palace, Brian O'Nolan (also a columnist recruited by Smyllie), Seán O'Faoláin, Frank O'Connor and even occasionally Oliver St John Gogarty. In addition were the poets, including F. R. Higgins, Patrick Kavanagh, Séamus O'Sullivan, and Ewart Milne. Several of these became friends of Betjeman's and this was the perfect venue for exercising what would in the twenty-first century be termed "soft power".

Louis MacNeice, who had been at Marlborough with Betjeman dropped in occasionally as did Cyril Connolly who had been at Balliol when Betjeman was up at Oxford.

Frank O'Connor is now chiefly remembered for his collections of short stories but he also published two novels, some poetry and travel pieces, and several essays. Having suffered at the hands of his alcoholic father, Michael O'Donovan, it was unsurprising that he adopted his mother's name as a *nom de plume*. He grew up in extreme poverty in Cork city, joined the IRA in 1918, was imprisoned at Gormanston Camp by the Free State and, after his release in 1923 became acquainted with W.B. Yeats, AE Russell and Lady Gregory, through whom he became involved with the Abbey Theatre of which he became managing director in 1937. He married the Welsh actress, Evelyn Bowen in 1939. Betjeman would have encountered him on his visits to the Pakenhams who were key movers in the development of Dublin theatre. O'Connor spent much of the 1950s lecturing in the United States, where he was divorced and re-married (later to create a slight ecclesiastical impediment when he was to give a lecture at Maynooth seminary) until he had a stroke at Stanford University in 1961. He returned to Dublin where he died five years later. Betjeman had a high opinion of his talents; in a letter to Oliver Stonor in March 1943, he wrote: "I see Frank O'Connor quite a lot. He is the best writer here. Very frustrated and unhappy and pro-us". In 1951 John Betjeman arranged to get O'Connor invited to join him on a BBC wireless show, "Poetic Licence".

Others whom he met in Dublin and might have encountered in the Palace Bar included: Jack Yeats, the artist and brother of the poet whom Betjeman had met in 1926 when they travelled together to Galway (W. B. Yeats died shortly before Betjeman was posted to Dublin), Terence de Vere White (who would often spend weekends with his wife at Collinstown House with the Betjemans), the poet Austin Clarke, Flann O'Brien, Maurice Craig, Cyril Cusack and, although possibly not in the Palace Bar, the brilliant polymath Father Paddy Browne (also and later known as Mgr de Brun) mathematician, classical scholar, translator and above all a poet who wrote some of the greatest poems in Irish of the twentieth century.

He was later to become President of Galway University. One of the relatively few happy photographs of Betjeman together with his son Paul shows them on an Irish beach when they were visiting Father Browne in 1948.

There were three Browne brothers of Cappoquin who went on to become priests: Paddy, Michael who became a cardinal, and Maurice Browne. Their sister was to marry Sean MacEntee, mentioned in the previous chapter (see p.76), who had fought with De Valera in the war for independence, was a founder member of Fianna Fáil, and a government minister during Betjeman's posting to Dublin. Maurice Browne wrote a fictionalised account of the Browne family (priests were restricted in publishing family memoirs at that time) under the pen name Joseph Brady. The book, *The Big Sycamore*, was published in 1958 and is a charming account of a way of life in rural Ireland which had all but disappeared by the time of publication, except in a few isolated areas of Connaught. This self-reliant culture; a couple of cows, a thatched cottage, a small fishing boat, was to vanish completely when Ireland joined the Common Market and the donkeys which had brought turf from the bogs ended up in tins of dog food.

In 1942, John Betjeman was instrumental in getting published an Irish number of *Horizon* (the literary magazine published in London from 1939-1950) and used it to publish and promote his friends: M. J. MacManus, L. T. Murray, Seán O'Faoláin, Frank O'Connor, Edward Sheehy, Jack Yeats and Patrick Kavanagh. He was good at making friends.

Paddy Kavanagh became a close friend, and celebrated their friendship in a poem he composed for the first birthday of the Betjemans' daughter, Candida, born in Dublin's Rotunda hospital. Betjeman had helped Kavanagh with getting his poems published in England in two literary journals both edited by friends of Betjeman; John Lehmann and Cyril Connolly. More importantly than this, they shared an affection for the poetry of place. Betjeman particularly admired Kavanagh's sense of place in the poem which was eventually to become *The Great Hunger*, his most famous poem, published in 1942.

Almost an exact contemporary of John Betjeman, Kavanagh was born in Co. Monaghan, the locus of several of his best known poems. Due to a scandal, his father had to leave and the family settled in Tullamore. He eventually moved to Dublin and had work published in local magazines and newspapers. When he joined a lending library, the first book he borrowed was T. S. Eliot's *The Waste Land*; Eliot as we have seen (see p. 29) was at one time a teacher of Betjeman at his prep school, became a friend and remained one for life.

Kavanagh published his first collection *Ploughman and Other Poems,* in 1936, an unsentimental observation of the reality of rural life. It was not enthusiastically reviewed at the time. The *Spectator* commented: "like other poets admired by A.E., he writes much better prose than poetry. Mr Kavanagh's lyrics are for the most part slight and conventional, easily enjoyed but almost as easily forgotten."

Fame first came to him when he published his first novel in London (where he had temporarily moved) in 1938; partly because of the publicity generated when Oliver St John Gogarty successfully sued him for libel, alleging the book referred unflatteringly to both his wife and his mistress.

Back in Dublin during the Second World War, Kavanagh was always broke. On one occasion Betjeman gave him £2, not a great sum even then, which inspired Kavanagh to write a sequence of two sonnets of thanks which begin:

> "Sonnet, tell all the things that can be done
> With this pound. Don't mention bread and cheese
> Or rashers for the breakfast, for not by these

Patrick Kavanagh
(ELINOR WILTSHIRE, NATIONAL LIBRARY OF IRELAND)

> Alone is the poet fed. Tell to John
> About the simple unmeasurable fun"

The friendship did not last much beyond the end of the war, perhaps because of Kavanagh's continual demands, but Betjeman clearly admired his poetry. Kavanagh's career was erratic and often alcohol fuelled until the last years of his life when he found his poetic muse again. He was fortunate for many years to enjoy the support of John Charles McQuaid, Archbishop of Dublin.

The journalist Emmanuel Kehoe wrote: "As a teenager I'd nourished a natural Irish anti-clericalism and anger at the sex-denying Catholic Church by reading his staggeringly powerful poem, *The Great Hunger*. Yet even this epic exercise in savage indignation did not lose Kavanagh the patronage of the Blackrock Borgia, the Archbishop of Dublin, John Charles McQuaid. What this ostensibly austere Spiritan found to admire and support in the raggle-taggle character who sometimes sounded like a latter-day William Blake long puzzled me, except that McQuaid must have seen in him a deep and authentic Catholicism."

In a short verse to his old friend John O'Dea written in 1965, Betjeman wrote satirically about ecumenism, referring to St Mary's Chapel of Ease by Parnell Square:

> The Black Church's pinnacles need never fall
> Its stones will proclaim in the loudest of hymns
> McQuaid is at last in communion with Simms

Betjeman became involved with the nascent movement to protect fine examples of Irish architecture and continued his stays at Gothic Revival houses: Woodbrook near Portarlington, home of relations of Penelope, Dunsany Castle in Co. Meath, Caledon in Co. Tyrone. We will return to the Gothic Revival in Ireland in a later chapter (see p. 101).

In a letter to Piper quoted earlier, he also wrote: "I am quite interested in Early Gothic Revival here. There is a Protestant chapel to a female Orphanage which is rather good – narrow gas pipes, fluted columns, queer capitals and grey and white colours". The building was by the architect, William Farrell, and was subsequently demolished.

His daughter, Candida, opined that "John Betjeman's greatest friend and kindred spirit during those Dublin years was the poet, Geoffrey Taylor". He had written two collections of poetry before the outbreak of the war; one he had withdrawn from publication because he was concerned by its anti-Catholic sentiment, the other was published under a pseudonym. His life up to and after the war was complicated; Taylor fell for the poet Laura Riding, who was the mistress of the poet and author Robert Graves. That ended Taylor's marriage to Norah McGuinness. This unsettled Graves's marriage to Nancy, who subsequently became Taylor's mistress, while Graves and Riding went to live in Spain. The relationship with Nancy was superseded by a relationship with Mary Dilwyn, to whom Nancy had introduced him; clearly these complicated changing ménages exhausted the poetic muse as Taylor spent the rest of his life editing anthologies.

Taylor and Betjeman continued to work together after the war. In 1955, commissioned by Faber to produce an anthology of love poetry, he immediately involved Taylor and was stricken when Taylor succumbed to a heart attack the following summer.

Brian O'Nolan, who wrote novels under the name of Flann O'Brien, journalism under the name of Brother Barnabas, and a long running column, "Cruiskeen Lawn" under the name of Myles na gCopaleen, until his premature death at the age of fifty-five, was one of the brightest fire-works of the Dublin literary scene. Born in Tyrone and taught by the future Archbishop McQuaid at Blackrock College, a prominent Dublin school, he wrote some extraordinary books which were a precursor of the magical realism of Gabriel García Márquez and Umberto Eco. His books sparkle and fizz with a sense of the absurd, in an inimitable Irish style which must have greatly appealed to Betjeman's own sense of the absurd.

John Charles McQuaid
Archbishop of Dublin

This association, lunches, dinners, drunken friends driven home in the embassy car, with poets, painters and writers were what Betjeman most enjoyed in his posting to Dublin. Apart from the Palace Bar, other favourite meeting places were Jammet's, a famous French restaurant which, in an act of gastronomic desecration was later turned into a Berni Inn, and the Buttery Bar in the basement of the Royal Hibernian Hotel, now turned into a shopping arcade.

George, who presided over the Buttery for fifty years was described by Patrick Campbell, listening to "fashionable Dublin matrons… I heard one lady, turkey-red around the neck, with her elbow in a dish of olives, say to George, 'The best chance you'd have of a bit of love in Dublin would be if the fella fell over you in the car-park.' George replied,' I am deeply distressed to hear that Madam'." George, with his wall eye and immaculately starched white tunic top, remained as ever diplomatic when I used to visit the Buttery as an undergraduate at Trinity Dublin.

A photograph taken at this time shows Penelope sitting next to the portly figure of R. M. Smyllie as she drove a horse and trap past the Palace Bar. Her husband, Betjeman is among a group standing on the pavement. In retrospect that may have been one of the happier moments of their life together.

Cyril Connolly, a friend of Betjeman's for many years, visited Dublin on a trip arranged by Betjeman in 1941, and wrote a memorable description of the snug in the Palace Bar as "warm and friendly as an alligator tank; its inhabitants, from a long process of mutual mastication, have a leathery look, and are as witty, hospitable and kindly a group as can be found anywhere."

In the summer of 1945, back in Garrard's Farm in Uffington, Betjeman wrote to Geoffrey Taylor: " I shall never live in London again. It is death. Curious hangovers from Eire survive – Ewart [Milne], Muriel MacSweeney and one or two dim Trinity men appear here. I see that till I die Eire is part of me".

THE GOTHIC REVIVAL

The Stately Homes of England,
How beautiful they stand,
To prove the upper classes
Have still the upper hand;
Though the fact that they have to be rebuilt
And frequently mortgaged to the hilt
Is inclined to take the gilt
Off the gingerbread

Noel Coward 1928.

Noel Coward was to write to Betjeman in 1961 praising him for his verse autobiography, *Summoned by Bells.*

Three years before Coward wrote this, John Betjeman paid his first visit to Ireland in the company of Pierce Synott and Maurice Bowra, staying at the Synott family home, Furness, scene of the attempted seduction of Synott by Bowra we mentioned in the Introduction (see p. 31). Betjeman had got into Oxford with difficulty, and was to have equal difficulty in graduating, but while at Magdalen he showed a talent for developing friendships many of which were to last a lifetime. In particular he became friends with a coterie of Irish aristocrats and gentry whose homes he visited.

It has been observed that in Evelyn Waugh's novel *Brideshead Revisited*, Charles Ryder is not so much in love with Julia, Lord Marchmain's daughter, as with Brideshead the house. The same is true of Betjeman; while he became good friends with some of the owners of the stately homes where he stayed, his interest in architecture, and particularly the Gothic Revival, was keener than his fascination with the aristocracy. The owners were the gilt but the houses were the gingerbread to pursue The Master's metaphor.

Betjeman had already become interested in architecture, particularly churches, when he was at the Dragon School. He used to bicycle around Oxford with his friend Ronald Wright (later to become a Catholic priest) and with a teacher, Mr Haynes (nick-named Tortoise Haynes because he taught us), who took him for rides on his motor-bike to visit early English Gothic churches. The same enthusiasm continued in school holidays in London where he would explore the rich heritage of the mediaeval churches hidden in the byways and alleys of the City of London, and in family holidays in Cornwall.

After a few difficult years as an indifferent teacher in various prep schools, Betjeman's first real employment to fill him with enthusiasm was working on the *Architectural Review*. Here he began to develop his views on architecture and his abominations ("Come friendly bombs and fall on Slough"). Central to his love of buildings was the Arts & Crafts movement and the Gothic Revival. Things Gothic had become popular in the late eighteenth century with Gothic novels, so wonderfully parodied by Jane Austen in *Northanger Abbey* but it saw its most visible manifestation in the passion for rebuilding houses as mock Gothic castles, the new Palace of Westminster after the fire, designed by Pugin, the high priest of the Gothic Revival, and in ecclesiastical buildings, which was to persist until the late Victorian era.

The Gothic Revival began in England and was firmly rooted in Anglo-Catholicism, drawing its inspiration from the great churches of the Middle Ages built *ad maiorem Dei gloriam*. The more severe forms of Protestantism frowned on all decoration or embellishment in churches as idolatrous and, in the form of Puritanism, had destroyed such ornamentation wherever they could. New churches were built with plain glass windows, white walls and square, forbidding lines. The Gothic Revival was a reaction against this dour simplicity and unsurprisingly connected with the Oxford Tractarian movement which leaned more towards Rome. Colour, castellations, icons, rood screens; a flamboyance which was deliberately designed to make a sensual appeal.

It coincided with the building of many Catholic churches in Ireland complete with mosaics, side chapels and richly coloured Munich glass, alluded to in one of John Betjeman's Irish poems quoted earlier.

It spread to Europe and in time to the Americas; in Ireland it led to the re-construction of many family homes as Gothic turreted castles. There are 14 notable churches in Ireland built in the Gothic style and a larger number of domestic dwellings ranging from a small castle such as Rosturk on the edge of Clew Bay to the grandeur of Ashford Castle or Dromoland Castle further down the west coast of Ireland. One of the finest examples is Lismore Castle, the Irish home of the Dukes of Devonshire, to which we will return later in this section (see p. 117).

Lismore Castle

A few remain in the hands of the original families; many fell into disrepair and were demolished, to add to the long list of those burned to the ground during the Troubles. Several, such as Ashford Castle and Dromoland, have become hotels while others have been bought privately as the twilight of the Ascendancy (see p. 120) became night.

When Betjeman thought of moving to Ireland in 1938, Constantia Maxwell, an historian and the first woman professor at Trinity College Dublin, wrote to him, "You would enjoy Ireland for 6 months, then you would begin to get melancholy, & long for English intellectual society". Whether she was right or not, the pleasure Betjeman derived from staying in some of the great houses of Ireland was unalloyed.

Soon after moving to his diplomatic posting in Dublin, he became involved with the Advisory Committee for the Recording of Irish Architecture. Together with Eleanor Butler (later the Countess of Wicklow), Harold Leask and others. Betjeman was instrumental in saving the Murray Collection of Francis Johnston's architectural drawings and ensuring it became the core of the collection in the National Library of Ireland. This is augmented by the Longfield collection of estate maps, the earliest of which dates to 1799. Betjeman found time to write essays and give lectures on Irish architecture as part of his work as Press Attaché.

It is worth noting a few of the houses in Ireland which captivated Betjeman's mind on his many visits there. I have avoided a superfluity of detailed description of machicolations and moats because these have all been better described by scholars of architecture, do not feature significantly in his poetry and the reader might find rather dull a quasi National Trust guide.

Furness House, near Naas and thus not far from Dublin, was acquired by the Synott family in 1897. It is a handsome Palladian mansion built in 1740 for Richard Nevill MP for Wexford. The Synotts extensively restored the house which retains original ornamental plasterwork and classical ceilings, and spacious reception rooms. In the surrounding parkland lie the ruins of a church dating back to the Dark Ages; no doubt this particularly appealed to John Betjeman's taste for ecclesiastical ruins.

At the time of writing, Furness had been put up for sale by the current owner, Patrick Guinness. Coincidentally, his grandfather, Bryan Guinness, later Lord Moyne was also a lifelong friend of Betjeman's and a fellow undergraduate at Oxford, and his grandmother, Diana Mitford, was one of the Mitford sisters to become close friends of

John Betjeman. Bryan and Diana Guinness lived near the farm house which the Betjemans rented for several years at Uffington in Berkshire and they were frequent visitors to each other's houses.

Another of the Mitford sisters, Deborah, was to marry Andrew Cavendish, the man who would in 1950 become the 11th Duke of Devonshire, brother of Lady Elizabeth Cavendish, Betjeman's "other wife" as his daughter, Candida, described her. One of the charming letters written when John Betjeman and Elizabeth were staying at Lismore Castle contains a passage in which Elizabeth exhorts John "to stop playing with Andrew" her ducal brother, and get on with writing poetry.

The Synotts sold Furness and Pierce Synott died in the unlovely county of Middlesex in 1982, far removed from the fertile meadows of Co. Kildare.

On the same excursion to Ireland, John Betjeman also visited the house of another Oxford friend, Cracky Clonmore, later the 8th and penultimate Earl of Wicklow. Known in Dublin literary circles as Billy Wicklow, he was banned from the family home, Shelton Abbey, because of his habit of attending Mass with one of the maids, an activity bordering on the treasonable for a Protestant peer.

Cracky Clonmore, by then the Earl of Wicklow, continued to update Betjeman with news from Ireland and their mutual acquaintances there until his death in 1978.

The house, an imposing Gothic revival castle built in 1819, made a strong impression on John Betjeman: "The entrance to Shelton Abbey was the dream of the Gothic Revival, and all I could wish... I'd never seen such luxury and splendour – rolling parkland down to the river at Woodenbridge, the Meeting of the Waters. It was paradise".

William Cecil James Philip John Paul Howard Clonmore, 8th Earl of Wicklow (BASSANO LIMITED)

Long after this first visit, Billy Wicklow, who inherited the house in 1946. was to try to turn Shelton Abbey into a hotel but the enterprise failed, he sold Shelton Abbey in 1950, and he spent his last years in a flat in Dublin. He and Betjeman were very close friends although as Billy Wicklow began his journey towards Rome, they drifted apart. Shelton Abbey in Co. Wicklow is now a prison, without doubt the most beautiful prison in these islands.

Birr Castle was the family home of another Oxford friend, Michael Rosse, to whom he wrote many letters. Birr Castle is another example of Gothic Revival in Ireland, the original castle having been rebuilt in the early nineteenth century, complete with towers, crenelations and lancet widows. The son of the Earl of Rosse responsible for rebuilding the castle was even more ambitious; he had built what was then the largest telescope in the world. Birr is an imposing building of more than eighty rooms, still owned by the Parsons family who have lived there for some twenty-five generations.

There is a charming manuscript letter in the Birr Castle archives in which Betjeman writes a thank you letter in verse, following one of his many stays there. Written from Pakenham Hall, the poem begins:

These castellations
Like constellations
And wide plantations
Mid scrags and moss
Do guard Birr Castle
A fine example
To all and sundry
Like the Earl of Rosse.

The original castle was raised in 1170 and from the thirteenth century for three hundred years was the home of the O'Carroll family. In 1620, the castle was granted to the Parsons family who began building a new castle adjacent to the site of the original castle. It was again rebuilt in 1641 after being attacked by Irish Catholic forces before its latest, and most ambitious, Gothic Revival re-modelling. One of the most striking features is the great entrance tower with a high lancet window above the portal. The extensive demesne was largely planted in the nineteenth century.

Betjeman became enamoured, as we mentioned, with the Gothic Revival movement while he was up at Oxford. The architect he came to most admire was Ninian Comper, the last of the great Gothic Revival architects, chiefly famed for his ecclesiastical work, fine tracery (celebrated by John Betjeman in verse) and stained glass. He took his inspiration from mediaeval architecture, designed chancels and reredoses and is best remembered for his re-introduction of the pre-Reformation "English altar" surrounded by riddel posts. Much though John Betjeman admired his buildings, he was disparaging about Comper's own mock Tudor house near Croydon when he visited it after the war. As he stayed in various stately, mostly Gothic Revival, homes in Ireland, Betjeman must have felt again and again that this was Elysium.

During a wartime visit to the West of Ireland with Penelope, at Tulira Castle, Betjeman fell in love with Emily Hemphill, (as described in an earlier chapter). Tulira Castle in Co. Galway was rebuilt in the high Victorian Gothic style in the 1880s by the Martyn (Hemphill) family. It is another collection of towers and battlements with its core being a fifteenth-century keep built by the de Burgo family. W.B. Yeats and Lady Gregory, who with

Edward Martyn founded the Irish National Theatre, were often visitors to Tulira. Yeats later fell out with Martyn because of the latter's Roman Catholicism; he wrote: "The whole system of Irish Catholicism pulls down the able and well-born if it pulls up the peasant… I used to think that the two traditions met and destroyed each other in his blood (Edward Martyn), creating the sterility of a mule". Having re-built Tulira, Lord Hemphill switched allegiances to the Celtic Revival under the influence of Yeats and Lady Gregory and later regretted that he had not chosen this style. Just before Easter in 1947, Betjeman, still keen to find a house for Evelyn Waugh in Ireland, wrote to Waugh suggesting that he should buy Tulira Castle. The former Kildare Street Club in Dublin, headquarters of the Ascendancy, is built in the same style as Tulira.

Edward Martyn was a deeply pious Catholic who used to write to the Pope to find out whether he could read books on the Index of proscribed texts. Apart from his interest in theatre, he was also very musical; he founded a Palestrina choir in Dublin and had an organ installed in Tulira Castle.

When the Betjemans were back in England after the war, Penelope named her Connemara mare Tulira; clearly she had forgiven her husband for falling in love with Emily.

Despite Yeats's reservations about his former friend, Tulira is a fine example of Gothic Revival, the only notable secular building designed by George Ashlin, the architect of the Cathedral at Cobh. It has a similar great tower entrance to Birr Castle (in fact it is remarkable how similar the Gothic Revival castles of Ireland are). The family sold Tulira Castle in 1982 and sadly many of the Gothic Revival furnishings were dispersed.

It was another Oxford friend, Basil Ava, the Marquess of Dufferin and Ava, who invited Betjeman to stay in his family home, Clandeboye House in Co. Down. Unlike most of the houses mentioned above, Clandeboye House is a classic, plain, square, Georgian mansion built in 1801 on the site of an earlier house. John Betjeman was strongly attracted to Basil Ava but Clandeboye did not have the comforts of the other stately homes in which Betjeman stayed in Ireland. Basil's grandfather, the first Marquess, had a distinguished diplomatic career, culminating in being successively Governor-General of Canada and Viceroy of India, but his diplomatic distinction was not matched by financial acumen.

Debts and family misfortune had led to Clandeboye being quite run down. Basil's daughter, Lady Caroline Blackwood, described it in her novel as damp infested with mushrooms growing from the ceilings, poor plumbing, cold and unappealing food. To add to this palpable decay, rather to Betjeman's taste, was the presence of Basil's mother, Brenda. She was convinced her son and daughter were changelings, snatched by malevolent spirits. She and John Betjeman enjoyed talking with each other about fairies.

Her connections with the real world were to help Betjeman in one of his early jobs, when on her recommendation, he was given the job of secretary to the Irish politician, Sir Horace Plunkett. Sir Horace was almost as eccentric as Lady Dufferin, Betjeman did not distinguish himself as a secretary, and the employment was short-lived. Sir Horace returned to his life-time obsession, a twenty volume history of the Irish agricultural co-operative movement, with a more suitable amanuensis.

In the late 1950s while Betjeman was on holiday with his mistress, Elizabeth, in Bavaria, Penelope took their two children, Paul and

Candida, to stay with Basil Ava's widow, Maureen Dufferin, mother of the last Marquess beside whom she is buried at Clandeboye.

Basil Ava remained a dear friend of John Betjeman's until his death in the Burma campaign in the last year of the Second World War. The title became extinct after the death of his only son and the house was eventually transferred to a trust financed by Guinness funds; Maureen was born a Guinness and was the first woman to sit on the board of the brewery.

The estate, covering 2,000 acres has a fine collection of trees and shrubs, together with beautiful formal gardens. In the estate is a charming folly, known as Helen's Tower. If you visit the battlefields of Flanders, one of the most important sites is the Somme. Here at 7.30 in the morning on the first day of the Battle of the Somme in 1916, the Ulster Division was the first in action, breaking through three lines of German defenses until, lacking reinforcements, they were pushed back. Their casualties were terrible; five years later, as the Ulster Division's training grounds were near Clandeboye, a replica of Helen's Tower was built at Thiepval by the battlefield. Gothic follies are falling out of fashion; Lord Berners, friend and neighbour of the Betjemans, built one of the last at his home, Faringdon.

Betjeman commemorated his friend, Basil, another gallant Ulsterman who fell in battle, in his finest elegiac poem:

"In Memory of Basil, Marquess of Dufferin and Ava"

On such a morning as this
with the birds ricocheting their music
Out of the whelming elms
to a copper beech's embrace
And a sifting sound of leaves

from multitudinous branches
Running across the park
to a chequer of light on the lake,
On such a morning as this
with 'The Times' for June the eleventh
Left with coffee and toast
you opened the breakfast-room window
And, sprawled on the southward terrace,
said: *"That means war in September."*

Friend of my youth, you are dead!
and the long peel pours from the steeple
Over this sunlit quad
in our University city
And soaks in Headington stone.
Motionless stand the pinnacles.
Under a flying sky
as though they too listened and waited
Like me for your dear return
with a Bullingdon nose of an evening
In a Sports-Bugatti from Thame
that belonged to a man in Magdelen.
Friend of my youth you are dead!
and the quads are empty without you.

Then there were people about.
Each hour, like an Oxford archway,
Opened on long green lawns
and distant unvisited buildings
And you my friend were explorer

> and so you remained to me always
> Humorous, reckless, loyal –
> my kind heavy-lidded companion.
> Stop, oh many bells, stop
> pouring on roses, and creeper
> Your unremembering peal
> this hollow, unhallowed V. E. Day, –
> I am deaf to your notes and dead
> by a soldier's body in Burma.

It was at Pakenham Hall (re-named Tullynally Castle in 1961) that Betjeman spent some of his happiest times in Ireland. The Pakenham family, Earls of Longford, were a creative, artistic, energetic family who embraced the new, independent Ireland. Betjeman was a contemporary at Oxford of Edward Pakenham, later Earl of Longford and a prolific author.

The Pakenham family originally acquired the estate in the aftermath of the Cromwellian wars in Ireland. Following the fashion, they remodelled their home in the Gothic Revival style, not once but twice in 1802 and 1840. It is an imposing castle in the flat countryside of Co. Westmeath with two large wings and more than 120 rooms. At the time of the first nineteenth-century re-building, it was said to be the largest castellated building in Ireland. Tullynally Castle is a typical example of Gothic Revival with turrets, towers, embellishments and battlements. John Betjeman wrote many letters from Pakenham Hall in the course of repeated happy stays there.

South of Tullynally Castle, Woodbrook House near Portarlington had been in the family of relations of Penelope's since the seventeenth century (the Chetwood-Aitkens). It was here that Jonathan Swift, Dean of Christchurch Cathedral in Dublin, wrote most of *Gulliver's Travels.* When the Betjemans were staying at this handsome Georgian House (a brief relief from Gothic Revival) in 1942, Betjeman was delighted, as he wrote to Cyril Connolly, to find: "a book signed by Swift and with his notes in it in an attic. The house is rambling, the demesne weed grown with a choked lake and all around bog and burnt-out houses in this the dimmest county in Oreland [Kildare]. It is my only convalescent home over here."

Yet further South, Dromana House sits on the River Blackwater near Waterford. The Blackwater is a well-known salmon fishing river which winds its way through the Waterford countryside, attracting many builders of stately homes to choose their spot on its banks.

Originally the home of a Fitzgerald heiress and of the Stuarts, connected by marriage to the Villiers family, Dromana House has been in the same family's hands for several centuries. The original castle was knocked down and the house rebuilt in the late eighteenth century with a fine Hindu Gothic arched gate lodge. Although the Georgian house was demolished in 1960, the house still remains in the possession of the original family, connected to that Emily Hemphill, later Villiers-Stuart, by whom John Betjeman was so smitten, in Galway, in the early years of the Second World War.

Betjeman also met Emily at the family's fishing lodge, the Yellow House at Helvick Head. Barbara Grubb, step-grand-daughter of Emily, who lives in Dromana House, was quoted in an interview with the *Irish Times*, after revealing that Greta Hellstrom was indeed Emily: "During his time in Ireland he met my step-grandmother, Emily. He visited her both in Galway and here in Co. Waterford.

They spent many happy times both at Dromana and at the Yellow House at Helvick. He wrote 'Ireland with Emily' after a bicycle ride through the Burren with her in the summer of 1943."

There is some debate about this first point as a manuscript version of the poem discovered in 2014 suggests the poem "A Unionist's Farewell to Greta Hellstrom" was written for Greta Wyndham, wife of Betjeman's friend, Dick Wyndham, a keen espouser of flagellation, and that he delayed publication of the poem for many years, until Dick's death, to spare his friend's feelings.

In 1974, replying to a correspondent, Mrs Noonan who had questioned him on the identity of Greta Hellstrom, Betjeman wrote: "I did meet a lady on a wet day in Dungarvan when she was staying in Helvick and I in Dublin" which might tilt the debate in favour of Emily as Greta.

Fair Day in Dungarvan (ROBERT FRENCH,
LAWRENCE PHOTOGRAPH COLLECTION,NATIONAL LIBRARY OF IRELAND)

Further down the river Blackwater is Lismore Castle, the Irish home of the Dukes of Devonshire, one of the grandest extant Gothic Revival houses in Ireland. Originally the site of Lismore Abbey, an important seventh-century monastery, Henry II ordered his son king John to build a castle on the site. This became the home of the Earls of Desmond until they lost their estates during the Elizabethan plantation of Ireland. Sir Walter Raleigh briefly owned it (as he did several other places) until he was imprisoned for High Treason, when he sold it to another great colonialist, Robert Boyle, who was to become the first Earl of Cork. He made an extraordinary fortune and had fifteen children of whom the fourteenth, also Robert Boyle, was the man who went down in history as "father of chemistry and brother of the Earl of Cork". He propounded Boyle's Law, the constant relationship between pressure, volume and temperature. The Great Earl of Cork, in an age of oppressive landlords, was distinguished by his bad treatment of his tenants. He boasted that "the mere Irish no longer exist in my domain", but his rapacity was to the ultimate benefit of the Cavendish family.

The Cavendish family acquired Lismore, Burlington House (now the home of the Royal Academy), Chiswick House and other notable properties through the marriage of the future 4th Duke of Devonshire to Lady Charlotte Boyle, heiress of the Earl of Burlington and Cork.

In 1812, the 6th Duke, commonly known as the "Bachelor Duke" began a Gothic transformation on the grandest of scales. Starting with the architect William Atkinson for the first stage of ten years of rebuilding, he then employed the noted architect Sir Joseph Paxton who created the current skyline. The 6th Duke liked Lismore better than any of his other houses, which included Chatsworth, spent more and more time there, then engaged Pugin to turn the ruined chapel of the Bishop's Palace into a banqueting hall.

Betjeman stayed at Lismore several times with Elizabeth Cavendish. In April 1958 he wrote to Deborah, Duchess of Devonshire:

"My dear Debo,
No words of mine can express the joy of Lismore and my visit there – no words can properly express thanks, nor even could a bunch of orchids. Andrew [the Duke] polished elegant and missing nothing and Crax [William Wicklow] tightish, enormous and with a flower in his button hole and also missing nothing made a splendid contrast in the airport bar. I wonder what Andrew and he said to each other after Feeble [his affectionate name for Elizabeth Cavendish] and I left.... Love to Andrew, that great man, that prince among men and love to you dear, kind and beautiful Debo.... I have not yet had a proof from the old Protestant printer. I expect Irish Customs will hold it up as dirty readin' matter".

The proof was for the poem "Ireland's Own" or "The Burial of Thomas Moore". Browne was the printer at Lismore of whom John Betjeman was very fond.

Lismore Castle was described ironically by Betjeman in his poem "A Lament for Moira McCavendish" (which is presumably about Elizabeth), written about 1958 and originally published in a limited edition of twenty copies, in which he writes of her brother, the Duke of Devonshire's, splendid castle:

> Her brother's wee cabin stands distant from Tallow
> A league and a half where the Blackwater flows,
> And the musk and potato, the mint and the mallow
> Do grow there in beauty along with the rose

Much earlier, in August 1931, Betjeman had written to Camilla Russell, with whom he had enjoyed a fling: "I shall whisk you off to Ireland when the collapse comes and there two enormous eyes will roll around the emerald fields and purple hills and a cool hand will clasp my clammy one and together we will walk to the Lake Isle of Innisfree or Pakenham or Furness or Shelton Abbey. Darling I love you I love you I love you. Dorothea and Dorothea every day. It's hell. But my God it's exciting, ain't it duckie? Clean up your little face and go and be nice to everyone, because I love you and don't care what happens."

The combination of the places in Ireland he loved so well and of erotic excitement was a potent brew. Dorothea (Lady Russell) had discovered their liaison and sequestered Camilla at her country house.

Years later, guest of a Duke, sleeping with the Duke's sister, staying at the finest mock Gothic Revival castle in Ireland, for the son of a furniture maker from North London, if I may paraphrase an earlier poet, the bard of the Lake District, bliss was it in that moment to be alive but to be at Lismore was very heaven.

HOW TO GET ON IN SOCIETY

If the Palace Bar could serve as a metaphor for artistic Dublin, the headquarters of the Anglo-Irish were firmly rooted in the dining room of the Kildare Street Club and the drawing room of the Shelbourne Hotel, a short walk up the road on St Stephen's Green.

Mark Bence-Jones wrote a most enjoyable description of the decline of the landed gentry of Ireland in his book *The Twilight of the Ascendancy*. An equally charming but fictional description of this eccentric breed is to be found in *Good Behaviour* and other novels by Molly Keane; she was a lifelong friend of Elizabeth Bowen whom we mentioned earlier in the context of her reports from wartime Ireland (see p.84), and of Charlie Cavendish (second son of the 9th Duke of Devonshire and thus great uncle to Lady Elizabeth Cavendish) until his premature death in 1944 at Lismore Castle.

For the benefit of those readers who are unfamiliar with Irish history, a brief summary may help to establish the relevant context. The Norman conquest of England was followed, a century later, by the Norman invasion of Ireland, but over the centuries, while the Normans were originally confined to the Pale, the Norman invaders and the Celtic or Gaelic population inter-married and, much of the time, managed to live peacefully together. In part this was because there was no difference of religion. Following the Synod of Whitby, the ancient Celtic church which had sent monks across Europe founding monasteries, became broadly aligned with Rome. The Normans built churches and monastic foundations throughout Ireland; many of the Gothic ruins which so enchanted John Betjeman in Ireland were the remnants of these foundations. This accommodation was damaged when Henry Tudor, better known as Henry VIII, refused an annulment of his marriage to Catherine of Aragon by the Pope, instigated the Reformation. As an aside it is interesting that three Welshmen have had a profound impact on Irish history; Henry VIII through the Reformation, Oliver Cromwell through his savage wars and Lloyd George through Partition.

The Gaelic chieftains and Norman Irish combined forces to oppose the imposition of the Protestant religion, and the seeds of future enmity were further sown when Henry's daughter, Queen Elizabeth, following wars in Ireland, created the first modern plantation in which great estates were given to Protestant settlers, among them the poet Spenser, one time secretary to the Lord Lieutenant of Ireland. These struggles continued through the two Desmond rebellions and only ended (temporarily) with the Battle of Kinsale in 1601.

In the English Civil War, the Irish remained largely loyal to the Stuart King in return for which Oliver Cromwell, devastated Ireland in the 1650s and then rewarded his followers with yet more Irish estates. This was further exacerbated by the victory of the House of Orange in the person of King William at the Battle of the Boyne.

So, after this one-minute snapshot of Irish history, by the nineteenth century most of the estates; and many of the new landlords created through the plantations following wars, were often absentees, living on their English estates and exacting rent from their impoverished and dispossessed tenants though the hated figures of land agents, these landlords largely, but not exclusively, made up the Anglo-Irish Ascendancy. Thus, the estates and the great houses of Ireland were, for the most part, occupied by Protestant landowners, loyal to the Crown, while their tenants were Catholics who were excluded for the most part from government. The gap between them was immense; in terms of wealth, opportunity and where their loyalties lay.

As described by Lionel Fleming in *Head or Harp*, his memoir of childhood in a small Cork village, Timoleague, as the son of the Church of Ireland rector, in the years leading up to independence, even when the circumstances of members of the Ascendancy were relatively humble, the two parts of society hardly had any interaction.

The real point that Fleming makes is about divided loyalty; brought up in the Ascendancy, educated in England, but living later in Dublin, to what polity was his loyalty due? This theme is also most effectively explored in Barbara Fitzgerald's 1946 novel *We Are Besieged*.

The terrible effects of the famine in the late nineteenth century, so well described by Cecil Woodham-Smith and Patrick Hickey, had further destabilised an untenable situation. While the poor starved after the potato crop failed, many landowners continued to demand rent and evicted those unable to pay. Through death or emigration, Ireland lost nearly a quarter of its population in the short space of seven years.

The Anglo-Irish Ascendancy reached the apogee of power, according to Bence-Jones, in the first half of the nineteenth century. This was the time in which so many built great mock Gothic castles, as we discussed in the previous section. But the end was in sight for them; the Wyndham Land Reform acts had diminished their estates and therefore their incomes, although many did not adapt their spending to the new realities, while the pressure for Irish independence, initially led by a growing Protestant middle class, was growing.

Not only were their estates diminished but many invested the sums received for their compulsorily purchased lands unwisely. Most notable were the Fitzgeralds, Dukes of Leinster, the premier dukedom of Ireland, who lost almost all the compensation funds they were paid. Their Dublin residence was sold and is now the Irish Parliament; their country place, Carton House, was turned into an hotel and golf course after its sale, bemoaned as architectural vandalism.

The Anglo-Irish were characterised by their eccentricity both before and after the decline of the Ascendancy. It has been argued that the limited gene pool among Catholic peers had led to in-breeding but this idiosyncrasy was by no means confined to this group. Among those who had excelled in unusual foibles was Lady Caroline Lamb. Daughter of the Earl of Bessborough, she produced a son and heir and went on to have three more children by different fathers. She is chiefly remembered for her passionate affair with the poet, Lord Byron which scandalised even the tolerant society of early nineteenth-century London. Byron grew weary of her obsession with him, including sending him love letters containing her pubic hair, and was relieved when her husband brought her to live in Dublin (he was Irish Secretary in the Duke of Wellington's government) where, despite a hope that her behaviour would not be noticed, she continued to outrage society.

Perhaps it is not surprising that the same Duke of Wellington was reputed to have said, when asked if his Dublin birth made him Irish: "Just because one was born in a stable does not make one a horse". Whether this was actually said by Daniel O'Connell about the duke is less important than the fact that it illustrates a truth about the Anglo-Irish; seen as English in Ireland and Irish in England a sense of deracination may have fostered eccentricity.

Another notable example was the Lord Carbery in the nineteenth century who suffered from depression. In his home Castle Freke in West Cork, he was said to keep a loaded shotgun beside his place at the dining table and, when troubled by melancholy, would pepper the portraits of his ancestors with bird shot. This was perhaps not uncommon. The historian Leanda de Lisle noted: "The pictures that my father brought back from Ireland in the Seventies were riddled with bullet holes. His mother's family liked to blame this on the Troubles, but it was, in fact, a consequence of drunken after-dinner games." This was clearly part of a family tradition as de Lisle also relates that a drunken Maurice Hastings had slashed the family portraits by Kneller with a riding crop before taking a gun into the garden and blasting off the private parts of a statue of Apollo, all the while cheered on by the ever present Maurice Bowra.

Others included Lord Kilmorrey who liked to rehearse his own funeral by getting his servants to push him on a trolley from his house to his mausoleum where he was eventually laid to rest beside his mistress, Priscilla. One might add to their number the long list of the Irish Jacobite peerage, created by the Stuart claimants in exile and recognised only by France, Spain and the Papacy people by names such as Redmond, MacMahon, Bourke, Dillon,

Kenmare, Mountcashell and Tallow; names which echo down the centuries of Irish history.

Three years before John Betjeman first visited the country, Ireland had attained independence and the Ascendancy had lost most of their power and influence and in many cases their houses and estates.

Yet it was this very Ascendancy, whom Betjeman was to meet at Oxford, who formed his introduction to Ireland and influenced many of his romantic views of the country. While several of these were eminently sane, Betjeman was most fascinated by those who worthily maintained an Anglo-Irish tradition of extreme eccentricity.

Bryan Guinness (who belonged to the former group of the eminently sane) of the brewing dynasty, later Lord Moyne, and a grandson of the first Earl of Iveagh, became a lifelong friend. Guinness, a lawyer, poet and novelist, was sympathetic to Betjeman's literary ambitions and offered him the post of sub editor of the *Cherwell*, the Oxford university magazine. Guinness was briefly married to Diana Mitford (of the famous Mitford sisters of whom more later), with whom he had two children before she ran off with the British fascist leader, Sir Oswald Mosley. Guinness subsequently re-married and had a further nine children. He was a trustee and important patron of the National Gallery of Ireland for more than three decades. He and John Betjeman exchanged many letters and the latter confided some of his more intimate thoughts to Guinness. Betjeman mentions Guinness in a letter to Anne Rosse after the death of her husband Michael, Earl of Rosse in 1979. Betjeman and Guinness were friends from their early days at Oxford until the end of the Poet Laureate's life.

Another man who became a lifelong friend was the same Michael Parsons, Earl of Rosse, who was also up at Oxford with Betjeman.

He stayed at Birr Castle, home to the great telescope, in Co. Offaly several times. Not only did they share a passion for preserving beautiful old buildings, they both shared an interest in the somewhat faded Irish aristocracy. Here is Betjeman writing to Michael Rosse in September 1955 from his rooms in London:

"Dear Michael,
Of course I will join the Irish Peers Association. My bank is the very one at which it banks, a nice dim bank, like the peers.... Do you remember when a Sir Somebody Aylmer, a cousin of the peer found that his footman was an Irish baronet too, called Elchin, and advertised for a baronet as second footman and got one called Sir Thomas Moore O'Connell, the descendant of a Lord Mayor of Cork who was selling small coals in that city? As someone said 'We have often heard Cork called the Venice of Ireland, but have never heard Venice called the Cork of Italy'... It was a joy to hear from you...love to Anne, we'll get her a medal. Seán O'B."

They remained lifelong friends. In 1948 Betjeman composed a short, unpublished, verse about Michael Rosse's sister, Lady Bridget Parsons. She was a great beauty, supercilious and choosy of her friends, living at that time in a flat in Mount Street in Mayfair, where many admirers courted her, for the most part without success:

> Beautiful Lady Bridget
> What do you do in your flat?
> Ferret about and fidget,
> Polishing this and that?
> Or lie in a bed with Andre Gide
> And a cachet faivre in case of need
> And a Borzoi asleep on the mat.

John Betjeman had escorted Lady Bridget triumphantly from court after her acquittal on a drunk driving charge in which her defence was that the reason she had been seen swaying by a police constable was because she was wearing high heels and a tight evening dress.

Betjeman was amused by the routines adopted and rigidly adhered to by the aristocracy; writing to Patrick Kinross, he describes a conversation with Elizabeth Cavendish's grand-mother, the dowager Duchess of Devonshire: "When I asked the Dowager Duchess at Hardwick whether she had ever used Chiswick House [a great mansion on the West side of London] she said, 'Only for breakfasts'...when I asked whether she used Compton Place, Eastbourne she said: 'Always at Whitsun'."

One of the defining characteristics of the aristocracy was the degree to which they were inter-connected (and often in bred). The more members of this tribe one met, acquaintanceship therefore grew exponentially. Doris Delevingne came from humble origins but through determination came to share a flat in Mayfair in her early twenties with a girl friend. A *grande horizontale*, she bestowed her favours on many of the leading men of society, including Randolph Churchill and, it was rumoured, the King.

Lord Castlerosse became so enamoured of Doris that he married her. Castlerosse (Valentine Browne) was the eldest son of the Earl of Kenmare, precisely the sort of Irish peer who fascinated Betjeman; obscure and on the brink of extinction. Doris Castlerosse became a famous society hostess and continued to sleep with a variety of men, until her husband, the model for Mr Chatterbox in Waugh's *Vile Bodies* divorced her. He cited as co-respondent, Robert 'Mad Boy' Heber Percy, the lover of Lord Berners, a close friend of the Betjemans, whom we encountered earlier in these pages (see p. 74).

Whether Doris had an affair with Mad Boy is unclear; she did take him to Paris for a birthday present where she paid for him to flog a *poule de luxe*. Doris died in her beloved Mayfair, alone in a room at the Dorchester Hotel, of an overdose of barbiturates. The Earldom of Kenmare is now extinct and the family estate in Kerry, Castlerosse, has become an hotel.

By the time Betjeman became an adult, the power of the aristocracy, with the empire their families had once governed, had already reached late afternoon in England and was firmly in its twilight in Ireland. These days the relative status of a marquis or a baron is a matter of indifference to most people but in reality, for Betjeman the fascination was born of nostalgia for the quaint customs of the past with their rituals of precedence and the panoply of nobility; these could furnish inspiration for a poet.

Pierce Synott, of Furness House near Naas, was also a friend made at Oxford and it was at his home that Betjeman stayed on his first visit to Ireland. Like most of his Oxford friendships, this was to last through his life. After a distinguished career in the UK Civil Service, Synott retired to his Irish estates where he served as Chairman of the Kildare Archaeological Association and Chancellor of the Order of Malta in Ireland.

In 1972 Betjeman wrote to Synott from Padua, recollecting that "Yours was the first country house in which I stayed (excepting that of Ernie's friend Sir Harry Webb in Wales) and since then how many pairs of linen sheets have received my lustful limbs in what fine mansions. O thank you, dear old thing, for your kind and scholarly appreciation of Yours, Seán o Betjemán". John Betjeman was staying with Elizabeth Cavendish in Padua with the conductor,

Raymond Leppard, and Synott had written to him in Latin.

One of the most enduring Irish friendships that Betjeman made at Oxford was with Edward Pakenham, later 6th Earl of Longford. He stayed with the Pakenhams over several summers at Pakenham Hall, a house which was always full of family and guests, in which Betjeman's talent for amusing was greatly appreciated, never more so than at the annual tea party for the local school, he composed scurrilous verses on the local vicar, Father Mouritz, and on his host:

> I never liked the AArish
> I never cared a whack
> For a lot of skulking Paddies
> Who'd stab you in the back.
> But of all the stinking Aarish
> With which that land is cursed
> The bloody Earl of Longford
> Is just about the worst.

Clearly tongue in cheek. As Betjeman wrote to Patrick Balfour from Pakenham Hall in September 1930: "I think Longford is delightful – amusing, appreciative of our jokes and no loony."

Edward Pakenham's father was killed at Gallipoli and he succeeded to the late seventeenth-century Earldom while still a school boy at Eton. He was an unusual member of the Anglo-Irish Ascendancy as he supported Irish nationalism, learned Irish, and was nominated as a member of the 5th Irish Senate by the Taoiseach, de Valera. Although he remained an Anglo-Catholic member of the Church of Ireland, his brother Frank Pakenham, also a friend of Betjeman's, who succeeded to the earldom as Edward had no children, became a Roman Catholic and, even more unusually for a hereditary peer, sat on the Labour benches and served in a Labour Government.

Apart from his long involvement with the Gate Theatre in Dublin, Edward was also a poet, a classicist, the translator of many works of French literature and a playwright. One of his plays was titled *Ascendancy*, a subject of which he had personal knowledge. The friendship between Edward Longford and John Betjeman was close and enduring. When Betjeman announced that he was leaving Dublin in June 1943, Longford wrote: "This is a great blow and a sudden one. I haven't been thinking about much else this week. It will be an awful gap in my life". Through Longford, Betjeman made several other friends including Cyril Cusack and Cathleen Delaney, mentioned earlier (see p. 49).

Many members of the greatly talented Longford family became friends of Betjeman's: Christine, Edward's wife, his sister Lady Violet, who married Anthony Powell, the author, Frank, his brother, and Elizabeth, Frank's wife, the well-known historian whose biographies of Lord Byron and the Duke of Wellington are hugely enjoyable.

Betjeman's interest in the more eccentric fringes of the Irish aristocracy is evident in many of the poems mentioned in the first section of this book. His enthusiasm for peer hunting is illustrated by an occasion in 1930 when, staying with the Pakenhams at Pakenham Hall in Co. Westmeath, he set off to find a somewhat obscure peer named Lord Trimlestown whose seat was at Bloomsbury near Kells, under the pretext of asking him to sign a petition to prevent the destruction of places of worship in Dublin. They asked for him in the area but nobody had heard of him and, when they finally found his house, learned at the ruined gates by the lodge that Lord Trimlestown had left it fourteen years ago. "Four of his nine sisters

Tullynally Castle (PETER GAVIGAN)

are nuns and the rest have not married so well. I am so sorry," wrote Betjeman in a letter to Patrick Balfour, "On the way back, heart-broken and stricken, we found an interesting sight in the roadside, an old man who lived in a wheelbarrow with a mackintosh and umbrella over the top, all year round. He was deaf and drunk but not dotty. I think he was a brother of Lord Trimlestown."

"This is an early Gothic Palace in the remotest part of Ireland [Westmeath would not now be considered so remote], to right and left rise round towers...ruined abbeys, ruined castles and prehistoric camps. I am in heaven. John Betjeman."

Lord Trimlestown's title was more ancient than most, having been created in 1461; the current holder, the 21st Baron, has no heirs so the title will lapse on his demise, joining the long list of Irish peerages which have gone from the twilight into extinction.

Which is also the case with the Earldom of Wicklow. William

Evelyn Waugh
(CARL VAN VECHTEN)

"Cracky" Clonmore later 8th Earl of Wicklow, was also a close friend of Betjeman at Oxford. They were introduced to each other by Lionel Perry, whose family had known the Wicklows in Ireland for many years. Clonmore was one of the few people with whom John Betjeman was able to discuss his religious beliefs. When they met, Clonmore was training to be an Anglican priest at St Stephen's House, Oxford. As we have seen earlier, his was among the first Irish stately homes Betjeman was to visit and he returned there many times. Clonmore wrote to Betjeman in 1927: "but very nearly from the first time I met you, I wondered whether you were not meant to be a priest". He went on to write that he thought John Betjeman would be particularly good as a priest in a slum, an interesting insight from one who knew him so well but difficult to reconcile with John Betjeman's love of titles.

By 1932, Betjeman was writing to their mutual friend, Lionel Perry: "Cracky is so Roman Catholic that it is impossible to understand him". Not only did religious conviction come between them, which John Betjeman alludes to in two letters to Evelyn Waugh, but in 1933 Clonmore had advised Penelope Chetwode not to marry John Betjeman. With the benefit of hindsight this might have proved rather good advice. The engagement was (temporarily) terminated when Penelope was sequestered with an aunt in the South of France.

Clonmore also disapproved of the way John Betjeman treated his father, Ernie, from whom he had become estranged as a young man; perhaps wanting to distance himself from his humble roots. Nevertheless, Clonmore was a frequent visitor to Uffington, the Betjemans' village in the early years of their married life.

Betjeman's fascination with the aristocracy is evidenced in many of his Irish poems, as we have already seen and we shall conclude this section with one of his best-known poems. Nancy Mitford, famous for her novels about upper class life in the first half of the twentieth century, had become interested in the theory of Alan Ross, that social strata could be accurately identified by vocabulary; that some words are U and others non-U. She published a short book on this theme, *Noblesse Oblige*, to which one of the contributors was John Betjeman. This poem, "How to Get on in Society", was originally the subject of a competition in *Time and Tide* in 1951, in which the task was to identify all the social solecisms, or non-U words and phrases:

Phone for the fish knives, Norman
As cook is a little unnerved;
You kiddies have crumpled the serviettes
And I must have things daintily served.

Are the requisites all in the toilet?
The frills round the cutlets can wait
Till the girl has replenished the cruets
And switched on the logs in the grate.

It's ever so close in the lounge dear,
But the vestibule's comfy for tea
And Howard is riding on horseback
So do come and take some with me

Now here is a fork for your pastries
And do use the couch for your feet;
I know that I wanted to ask you –
Is trifle sufficient for sweet?
Milk and then just as it comes dear?

I'm afraid the preserve's full of stones;
Beg pardon, I'm soiling the doileys
With afternoon tea-cakes and scones.

One of the few people at Oxford who disapproved of Betjeman's social climbing was the poet W. H. Auden who felt this was not a proper occupation for a poet; perhaps his opinion of John Betjeman was coloured. Auden's biographer, Charles Osborne, claimed that the two poets slept together at Oxford. Betjeman being discovered in Auden's bed in the morning by his scout, the cleaner was bribed by Auden with £5 to keep quiet. Auden used to recount the story, concluding: "it wasn't worth the £5." However, the two men remained friends until Auden's death. Auden was instrumental in getting John Betjeman's *Collected Poems* published in America and wrote a generous preface.

Betjeman was well aware of his desire to improve his social status; it was a conscious thing. One of his poems (not included in the *Collected Poems*), expresses it accurately:

A single topic occupies our minds.
'Tis hinted at or boldly blazoned in
Our accents, clothes and ways of eating fish,
and being introduced and taking leave,
'Farewell', 'So long', 'Bunghosky', 'Cheeribye' –
That topic all-absorbing, as it was,
Is now and ever shall be, to us – CLASS

And on staying with Elizabeth's brother Devonshire in 1953, Betjeman wrote to Penelope: "Nooni, nooni, nuke, her hubby went off to stay with a Duke. Nibbly, nobbly, nibbly nob, her husband was clearly a bit of a snob."

John Betjeman's earliest connection with Ireland may have been a more modest one. When his father, Ernie, died in 1934, consternation was caused at his funeral by the arrival of a hitherto unknown second Mrs Betjeman (as she claimed) complete with family. Whether they were actually married or whether Ernie had just enjoyed a secret life with her, unbound by matrimony, in his will he left to Miss Norah Kennedy of Cappagh, Kilrush, Co. Clare the sum of £300. On one of John Betjeman's earliest visits to Ireland, Ernie insisted on accompanying him, chiefly it seems for the purpose of paying an unaccompanied visit to Miss Kennedy.

We have already written about his connection with Lady Elizabeth Cavendish who was his mistress for the last decades of John Betjeman's life. In his relationship with her, the daughter of a Duke, he ascended by association to the highest rung of the table of precedence. Lady Elizabeth was a lady-in-waiting to Princess Margaret; in Betjeman's latter years living in Chelsea he, Elizabeth and "Little Friend" as he referred to H.R.H., would go to church together. The son of a furniture maker from North London was consorting with royalty.

By the time John Betjeman died, Poet Laureate and Knight Commander of the British Empire, friend of the great, the sometimes good, and the titled, he had charmed his way into that gilded circle which had so entranced him when he had gone up to Oxford six decades earlier.

IRELAND IN VERSE

Betjeman was a traditionalist in almost every aspect of his being; his love for High Church Anglicanism, the Gothic Revival, old buildings, landscape and above all in poetry; both the poets who influenced him and the way he set about writing poetry. He eschewed the contemporary taste for blank verse in favour of the traditional rules of poetry; the iamb, the trochee and the spondee, the dactyl and the caesura, were music to his poetic ear.

By the time John Betjeman published his first poetry in the 1920s, Modernism in the world of art was in the ascendant. In art it expressed itself pre-eminently in dislocated body parts, in philosophy it had moved on from the rationalism of the Enlightenment to the post-modern concept that nothing is knowable (the subject of keen debates in the borderlands of philosophy and science between Heisenberg and Einstein, so wonderfully satirised by Schrodinger in his example of the cat, now sometimes taken as a serious scientific observation); in literature in such towering works as T. S. Eliot's *The Waste Land* and James Joyce's *Ulysses*, both published in 1922.

T. S. Eliot and e. e. cummings were among the apostles of Modernism in poetry. Those whose poetry has survived the test of time are, as always, poets with ideas to express in a memorable way, (including several modernists such as T. S. Eliot). Modernism however, for many of its proponents, meant little more than rejecting the poetic conventions of previous generations, the nineteenth century in particular. So, a graceless poetry came into being, devoid of scansion, rhyme, structure or original thought; often its only tenuous claim to be poetry and not prose was that the lines were of uneven length and syntax was ignored.

On to this stage stepped John Betjeman, a poet who consciously used the structures of poetry; rhythm, stanzas, rhyme, the conventions of verse of former generations. Within three decades after he first published his verse, his poetry was tremendously popular and naturally earned the ire of those who worshipped at the altars of Modernism, for whom Betjeman was a third rate, trite poet, rooted in the past in his approach to poetry and in his mourning of a bygone age, his love for Victorian buildings, and an hierarchical approach to society perhaps best summed up in the hymn "All Things Bright and Beautiful": "The rich man in his castle, The poor man at his gate, He made them, high or lowly, And ordered their estate."

Siegfried Sassoon
GEORGE CHARLES BERESFORD

While the exam syllabi include (deservedly) poets such as T.S. Eliot and Robert Frost, Seamus Heaney and Stevie Smith, W. B. Yeats and Siegfried Sassoon, there are very few instances in which a poem by

Betjeman is a set text. Perhaps his poetry was too entertaining and too popular; but is it good poetry; that is to say; does he say something worthwhile in a worthwhile way?

Philip Larkin was an admirer of Betjeman's poetry, precisely because of its intelligibility, a sentiment reciprocated by Betjeman towards Larkin's verse. Larkin's poetry was likewise decried by the Modernists and, although more than a generation apart the two poets became friends, first corresponding in 1958 and finally meeting three years later. Candida wrote of her father: "He used to read Larkin's poem 'The Whitsun Weddings' aloud so often that I got to know it by heart…he felt an affinity towards Larkin which he had never felt quite so keenly for his close friends Eliot, Auden, Blunden or Plomer". There were other parallels between the two poets; Larkin spent his life between two women, Maeve Brennan and Monica Jones, although he never married.

An avowed atheist, many of Larkin's poems are connected with religion, including "An Arundel Tomb", inspired by a visit to Chichester Cathedral with Monica Jones, and his last great poem "Aubade". Like Betjeman, the externals of religion fascinated Larkin; unlike Betjeman he did not let the essence of religion trouble him. When he lay dying, Maeve Brennan brought the Catholic chaplain of Hull University (where Larkin had been librarian for many years) to his bedside. When Larkin opened his eyes and saw the clerical figure, he expelled him in crude Anglo-Saxon, and revised his will. Removing Maeve as a beneficiary, he left all his (ever growing royalties) to Monica. As a final irony, she left her Larkin wealth for the maintenance of St Paul's Cathedral, Durham Cathedral and Hexham Abbey.

John Bayley in an essay in the *London Review of Books* in 1980, wrote of him: "Betjeman is a complete original: no other poet had perceived or expressed these things before, although the poetry is not concerned with being itself but is quite happy to be poetical and to borrow indiscriminately from poetic convention. In that, as in much else, Betjeman is like Wordsworth. The genuineness does not depend on a new style but on a new kind of perception, and in both poets there are 'two voices'. Wordsworth enjoying and Wordsworth expatiating are very different things, and the same is true with Betjeman. He is versatile; he has many tones; but only the passion rings true."

Betjeman had published three collections of poetry by the time he was posted to Dublin. His three years there were a fallow period, except for beginning the work which was later to become *Summoned by Bells*, published in 1960. However, as with every poet, the thoughts, themes and words that are part of everyday existence are not confined to one time or place but may flower years later. While a number of his poems are specifically Irish, they can be better understood as part of his overall work.

His poetic output was substantial and, like many poets, uneven in quality. Many of the poems contained in the *Uncollected Poems*, that is, those not selected by Betjeman or his publisher, Jock Murray, do not merit reading, but in those poems that were selected there is a handful which bear comparison with the best poetry written in English in the twentieth century. We have mentioned a number of these in the course of this book and among these, I think it would be fair to include at least one of his poems set in Ireland: "The Irish Unionist's Farewell to Greta Hellstrom in 1922".

Betjeman summarised his poetic inspirations in a letter to William Plomer in the summer of 1947: "I am a Church of

England Catholic. I love the Church of England. Sex, architecture, topography, seaside and fear of death are I suppose chief motives in my poetry".

The themes of his poetry are universal: love, lust, lament, admiration of beauty, despair, fear of mortality, religious doubt and place but he expressed them in a context which was uniquely Betjeman, what one might call his poem-scape. Pre-eminent in this poem-scape was place, as we discussed in the first chapter (see p.17). Open his *Collected Poems* at random and the pages are full of place names: Canterbury Gate, the Banbury Road, Kirkby with Muckby-cum-Sparrowby-cum-Spinx, Cricklewood, Henley; the beautiful, the banal, the euphonious, and the ghastliness of Slough, are all material for his verse. Sometimes the places are chosen for their sound, as those small villages of Lincolnshire; at times the place seems no more than a happy coincidence: "Her sturdy legs were flannel-slack't/The strongest legs in Pontefract" but the place has a point because it is the licorice fields of Pontefract which provide the setting for the kind of love affair in which Betjeman revelled:

> She cast her blazing eyes on me
> And plucked a licorice leaf;
> I was her captive slave and she
> My red-haired robber chief.
> Oh love! For love I could not speak,
> It left me winded, wilting, weak
> And held in brown arms strong and bare
> And wound with flaming ropes of hair

In the poem "Original Sin on the Sussex Coast", the place names are banal: Willow Way, Seapink Lane, the Garden of Remembrance, but they are important because they are the memorised map of escape for a small boy trying in vain to avoid a savage beating by the gang lying in wait for him:

> "You're to be booted. Hold him steady, chaps!"
> A wait for taking aim. Oh trees and sky!
> Then crack against the column of my spine,
> Blackness and breathlessness and sick with pain
> I stumble on the asphalt. Off they go
> Away, thank God, and out of sight
> So that I lie quite still and climb to sense
> Too out of breath and sense to make a sound.

The absence of rhyme is apposite to the seriousness of the subject; remembering as an older man the pain of the child; and what an effective metaphor is "climb to sense"; we almost miss it in the emotional moment.

In "Devonshire Street W1", the opulent, eighteenth-century street is used to set the scene for the couple who emerge oblivious to the sunlit splendour of the street, from a consulting room, because they only have one thing on their minds, the news he and his wife have just been given by the doctor:

> "Oh merciless, hurrying Londoners! Why was I made
> For the long and painful deathbed coming to me?"

And as they walk down Devonshire Street, the poem concludes with a charming bathos necessary to the terrifying imminence of death:

> She puts her fingers in his, as loving and silly
> At long-past Kensington dances she used to do

"It's cheaper to take the tube to Piccadilly
And then we can catch a nineteen or a twenty-two."

Lust is a frequent theme in Betjeman's poetry; explicitly in poems such as "Late Flowering Lust" and, remorsefully in "Senex", in which the final two stanzas evoke the end of "Bagpipe Music" by Louis MacNeice:

Get down from me! I thunder there,
You spaniels! Shut your jaws!
Your teeth are stuffed with underwear,
Suspenders torn asunder there
And buttocks in your paws!

Oh whip the dogs away my Lord,
They make me ill with lust.
Bend bare knees down to pray, my lord,
Teach sulky lips to say, my Lord,
That flaxen hair is dust.

There is lust in the Irish poems, most notably in Part II of "Sir John Piers", although here couched in a moving poetic speech of seduction, in which each line is broken by caesurae to prolong the anticipatory moment:

Lie still for ever
on this little peninsula,
Heart beat and heart beat
steady till we wake.

But there is love too, mingled with regret, most notably in "The Irish Unionist's Farewell to Greta Hellstrom in 1922." The poem is probably written to Emily Villiers-Stuart (rather than Greta

Wyndham) for whom Betjeman had a strong but unreciprocated love, which we have discussed in an earlier chapter (see p. 50).

> Had I kissed and drawn you to me,
> Had you yielded warm for cold,
> What a power had pounded through me
> As I stroked your gleaming gold!
> You were right to keep us parted:
> Bound and parted we remain,
> Aching, if unbroken hearted –
> Oh! Dungarvan in the rain.

The pain of a love unconsummated; the sense of regret, the sorrow of parting; all these are handled with simplicity and sincerity.

As we have seen, Betjeman charmed his way into the company of the upper classes by his talent to amuse and entertain. In Colonel Kolkhorst's salon, he was known as the clown. His success in his posting to Dublin was in large part due to his affability and talent to amuse. Most poets tend by their nature to be serious beings; there is no record of Wordsworth and Coleridge amusing each other in their long collaboration, and the closest John Keats came to a joke was when he discovered, on a walking holiday in the West of Ireland, that Irish miles are much longer than English miles. The great poetic figures of the recently ended Victorian age; Tennyson, Arnold and Browning took life, themselves and their poetry very seriously.

In contrast, in Betjeman's life and poetry, humour is never long suppressed, no doubt adding to the critical view that he was no more than a versifier because, would argue the po-faced prophets of post-Modernism, levity has no place in poetry.

Betjeman, because of his humour, was easy to parody: Anthony Burgess produced a *faux* Betjeman poem, combining religion and lust, in his novel *Earthly Powers*:

> Thus kneeling at the altar rail,
> We ate the Word's white peppery wafer.
> Here, so I thought, desire must fall,
> My chastity be never safer.
> But then I saw your tongue protrude,
> To catch the wisp of angel's food.

And a *Spectator* competition set by Jaspistos, contained a memorable couplet parodying "A Subaltern's Love Song":

> Miss Joan Hunter Dunn, Miss Joan Hunter Dunn;
> Take down your knickers and let's have some fun

While his poem "The Mistress", in which he fantasises about a beautiful woman he has observed while attending the Grosvenor Chapel with Elizabeth Cavendish, led to a burlesque in *Private Eye* by "the Poet Laureate Sir John Thribb":

> Lovely lady in the pew,
> Goodness, what a scorcher – phew!
> What I wouldn't give to do
> Unmentionable things to you.
> If old God is still up there
> I'm sure he wouldn't really care.
> I'm sure he'd say, 'A little lech
> Never really harmed old Betj'.

But the parodies miss the point; Betjeman never fails to capture emotion accurately, even when the shape of the poem is comedic.

Humour and love are, it has been claimed, the two emotions which make us human but we might have to back as far as Chaucer to find a poet like Betjeman who made it such an integral part of his verse. Shakespeare does jokes, but they tend towards the puns or scatology which would amuse the groundlings. Donne and Marvell play on metaphysical conceit with a certain dark humour, and from then onwards, with the possible exception of Alexander Pope, there is a long line of poets from Milton, totally devoid of humour (or love) to the scarifying poets of the First World War. What a relief to find a poet who knew how to love and laugh. We have discussed earlier examples of John Betjeman's sense of humour (see p. 23); a sense of humour which comes through in the Irish poems.

The humour in his verse says something important about Betjeman's qualities; he was a kind man; kind to those he met, kind in his efforts to those he never met. The humour is never barbed but sympathetic, even when it concerns the residents of Slough of whom he writes: "It's not their fault they do not know/ The birdsong from the radio". Which is why none of the parodies quite work because they are devoid of kindness.

The first of these Irish poems in the *Collected Poems* is about a serious theme, usury and religion, but in "An Impoverished Irish Peer", the tone is one of humour and the cadences are the soft Irish lilt (note the "do sing") which Betjeman so enjoyed imitating:

> Within that parsonage
> There is a personage
> Who owns a mortgage
> On his Lordship's land....
> Where the little pebbles do sing like trebles

As the waters bubble
Upon the strand…

As many flunkeys
As Finnea has donkeys
Are there at all times
At himself's command…
Yet if his Lordship
Comes for to worship
At the Holy Table
To take his stand,
Though humbly kneeling
There's no fair dealing
And no kind feeling in the parson's hand…

In his book, *Famine in West Cork*, Patrick Hickey quotes a few lines of verse attributed to Thomas Barry, parish priest of Schull about 1830 which might well have influenced Betjeman:

There was a parson
Who loved 'divarshun'
And ne'er was harsh on His flock so few…
The tithe was heavy
That he did levy
And he kept a 'bevy'
Of tithing men

Betjeman's delight in place, nostalgia, humour and the Irish speech rhythms are there again in "The Small Towns of Ireland" where he contrasts the tragic misfortunes of the former Lord whose mansion's a ruin:

His impoverished descendant is dwelling in Ealing
His daughters must type for their bread and their board,
O'er the graves of his forebear the nettle is stealing
And few will remember the sad Irish Lord

[With the present-day bucolic calm]:

I hear it once more, the soft sound of those voices,
When fair day is filling with farmers the Square,
And the heart in my bosom delights and rejoices
To think of the dealing and drinking done there

A similar image of a small country town on fair day is found in Patrick Kavanagh's poem "In Memory of my Mother" written in 1945 which would certainly have been read by his friend Betjeman; in common with most writers, he was, like Autolycus, a snapper up of un-considered trifles.

Place, lust, love, humour and of course one other defining human characteristic is that every self-reflective adult has thought about their own death; it is not surprising that the fear of death has informed poetry at least since King David wrote in Psalm 103: "As for man, his days are as grass: as a flower of the field, so he flourisheth. For the wind passeth over it, and it is gone; and the place thereof shall know it no more", and the poem-scape of many poets has been shaped by this. T. S. Eliot wrote of the dramatist Webster that he "was much obsessed by death and saw the skull beneath the skin". In Betjeman's poetry, the terror of death, despite his observant Christian faith, is never far away. He may treat it with disgust as in "Late-Flowering Lust" or with comedy in "Sun and Fun":

There was sun enough for lazing upon beaches,
There was fun enough for far into the night.

But I'm dying now and done for,
What on earth was all the fun for?
For I'm old and ill and terrified and tight.

And in Part IV of "Sir John Piers", these defences are stripped away and, as the returned exile awaits his demise, barricaded in his encumbered estates, cut off from human contact, feeling already entombed, the focussed thought is of the desolation that in death we are truly alone:

Blue dragonflies dart on and do not settle,
Live things stay not; though my walls are high,
They keep not out the knapweed and the nettle,
Stone are my coffin walls, waiting till I die

In his final TV programme series made by Jonathan Stedall not long before Betjeman died, Stedall asks him: "What do you fear most, John?" and John Betjeman replies: "…I remember hearing somebody say, 'Of course as a Christian I'm bound to believe in eternal life; but I prefer the idea of extinction'. That was a very good man said that. And I thought it was really the most awful thing you could say. And now I find it's true."

Where was the comfort of eternal rest in Betjeman's relationship with death? There is a faint hope perhaps, but not one of great immediacy, as the final one and a half stanzas of "Ireland with Emily" suggest:

Till there rose, abrupt and lonely,
A ruined abbey, chancel only,
Lichen-crusted, time-befriended,
Soared the arches, splayed and splendid,
Romanesque against the sky.

> There in pinnacled protection,
> One extinguished family waits
> A Church of Ireland resurrection
> By the broken, rusty gates.
> Sheepswool, straw and droppings cover,
> Graves of spinster, rake and lover,
> Whose fantastic mausoleum
> Sings its own seablown Te Deum,
> In and out the slipping slates.

Those lines alone, their sense of elegiac finality, the plangent chords, would seem enough to make Betjeman merit serious consideration as a poet.

Lord Alfred Douglas
GEORGE CHARLES BERESFORD

Betjeman agreed with Lord Alfred Douglas (Oscar Wilde's Bosie) that "good poetry is made up of two things; style and sincerity. Both are requisite in equal degrees".

He was quite conscious of the process of creating poetry and offers some interesting insights. In a letter in 1954, he wrote: "…a lot of the verses were written with tunes in my head, and certainly the dactylic group has 'Bonnie Dundee' as a basis, though probably '*Fête Champêtre*' comes from some [Thomas] Moore melody… I think the 'Irish Unionist's Farewell' was composed to the tune of 'Clementine', and you will find that 'Flight from Bootle' also goes to that tune. I have an idea that 'I love your Brown Curls' probably comes from Moore…tunes which are ringing through my head constantly are 'Hryfdol', 'Tea for Two', 'The Day thou gavest Lord has ended,' 'Now the Day is Over', 'Over the Sea to Skye,' 'Tom Bowling'…" It is easy to find these tunes and others in many of Betjeman's poems. They all have strong, simple melodic lines.

This is an important dimension of poetry; it may be written very privately but it is a form of communication which must stand the test of public performance, of poetry-reading. In July 1958, writing to his friend, and occasional poet, James Lees-Milne about some of his poetry, Betjeman writes: "That is observed, private thought made public… BUT I don't think any of them read out loud well. I have tried that. For instance 'The Dream' may look as though it keeps the rule of rhyme, but though it does, the rhymes are purely intellectual. You can't use rhythms or rhymes like that. A line should end as you speak. A really natural poem should need no punctuation; it should punctuate itself by the natural cadence of its words."

Betjeman was a punctilious user of punctuation but his poems stand the test of readability. Open the *Collected Poems* at random and, even where the metre is complex, the poems are a pleasure to read aloud.

An important part of the process of writing poetry is the pleasure of playing with words, using the unexpected word to create greater impact. He mentions in a letter of December 1956 how much he enjoys the private language of nineteenth-century church architects more than any language in the world; and this is the key: poets invent their own private language.

We find this word-playing pleasure primarily in the letters Betjeman wrote to Penelope, in which they had invented their own private language, based on an eclectic mixture of cockney and Irish speech rhythms, Greek and nonsense words. Writing to his wife in 1955 while he was with Elizabeth Cavendish, Betjeman composes:

> Much love moi own darlin
> Ijjus ayfevery oogli
> Sweet precious pointed-eaded
> Eccentric noonyish
> Own loovin Nibbly Plymmi
> From Yorz trewely, Tewpie

Which should qualify for inclusion in any anthology of post-Modern verse.

Of his direct contemporaries, T. S. Eliot and W. H. Auden, both friends and lifelong correspondents of Betjeman, would rightly rank higher in the critical pantheon of poets. Both, like Betjeman, had a substantial corpus of poetry, all tried ambitiously long poems, all dealt with the substantive matters of what it means to be human and all were masters of the metric form. Frost (except for one poem), D. H. Lawrence, Edward Thomas, Kingsley Amis, Ted Hughes and Ezra Pound have a dwindling following (as poets) but among those whose poetry is still enjoyed, names such as W. B. Yeats or Gerald Manley Hopkins, it is safe to say that Betjeman's poetry has stood the test of close to a century and still provides pleasure to readers around the world wherever poetry in English is read.

We will let Betjeman have the final word. He wrote to John Sparrow, who was later to become Warden of All Souls, in 1947: "[One of the themes of his poetry] an all-over picture of Ireland… today with Irish Catholicism dominant and the old Somerville and Ross Landlord Protestantism dead. Hence all the references to deserted demesnes and to the Sacred Heart and to the difference of Galway people from Midland (of Ireland) people. Essentially a Social as well as a Topographical poem... So too when you describe my 'amatory' poems really it would be better to call them 'sexy'. All my better poems are Amatory in that they are written from a love of the people and place they describe. They are written from love and, I like to think, reverential understanding."

ENVOI

The last few years of Betjeman's life were marked by declining health, difficulties with walking, and fear that his poetic muse had deserted him. Penelope spent much of her time in India and it was Elizabeth Cavendish who took care of him.

By now a knighted (1969) Poet Laureate (1972), John Betjeman had a vast acquaintance and an audience who wrote to him frequently. He continued to work hard, replying to every letter he received, serving as patron of numerous organisations and still going out to dinners and staying with friends both new and old.

Cyril Cusack sent Betjeman a telegram when he was made Laureate "About time too, your people knew that forests walked and fishes flew."

But it was the deaths of many of his oldest friends which taxed him most and among them many of his circle of Irish friends, Lionel Perry, Cracky Wicklow and many others kindled in him a nostalgia for that country which he had seen as the most perfect place on earth when he first visited Ireland in 1925.

In the chapter "Undercover in Dublin", I mentioned that soon after leaving Dublin he fell in love with a woman named Alice Hardy, his assistant at the Ministry of Information in Bath (see p. 73). They kept in touch and in a letter to her in 1981, John Betjeman wrote: "Stands Corkagh still under the grey Dublin sky? While Clondalkin awaits the ghost oá a train down to Kingsbridge, Does Rosemary [Colley] remember Mrs Madan? 'Wasn't she decoratin' the church and didn't she fall off the Holy Table?' How Penelope and I laughed about those dear old Church of Ireland days."

BIBLIOGRAPHY

Collected Poems, John Betjeman, John Murray, 1970

Harvest Bells: New and Uncollected Poems, Bloomsbury Continuum, 2019

John Betjeman, Letters, Candida Lycett Green, Methuen, 2006

Betjeman, A. N. Wilson, Random House, 2006

John Betjeman The Biography, Bevis Hillier, John Murray, (abridged), 2006

Betjeman A Life in Pictures, Bevis Hillier, John Murray, 1984

The Betjeman Society, various journals

Twilight of the Ascendancy, Mark Bence-Jones, Constable, 1987

Head or Harp, Lionel Fleming, Barrie & Rockcliff, 1965

Hitler's Irish Voices, David O'Donoghue, Somerville Press, 2014

Jammet's of Dublin, Maxwell and Harpur, The Lilliput Press, 2012

All Cultivated People, Patricia Boylan, Colin Smythe, 1988

Remembering How We Stood, John Ryan, Gill & Macmillan, 1975

In Time of War, Robert Fisk, M. H. Gill, 1983

The Emergency, Bernard Share, Gill and Macmillan, 1978

Patrick Kavanagh Man and Poet, ed. Peter Kavanagh, Goldsmith Press, 1987

Memories, Maurice Bowra, Weidenfeld & Nicolson, 1966

ACKNOWLEDGEMENTS

The publishers and author thank John Murray Hachette and PSClear for permission to quote from *Collected Poems*, John Betjeman,1970 and Methuen for permission to quote from *John Betjeman Letters*, Candida Lycett Green, 2006 and Bloomsbury Continuum, an imprint of Bloomsbury Publishing plc. for permission to quote from *Harvest Bells: New and Uncollected Poems*, John Betjeman, 2019.

The following links provide access to the licences under which a number of the photographs in this book have been licenced:

https://creativecommons.org/licenses/by-sa/1.0/

https://creativecommons.org/licenses/by/2.0/

https://creativecommons.org/licenses/by-sa/2.5/deed.en

https://creativecommons.org/licenses/by-sa/3.0/deed.en

https://creativecommons.org/licenses/by-sa/4.0/deed.en

The publishers have made every effort to trace all owners of copyright illustrative and text material. In the case of any omissions that have been unconsciously made the publishers apologise and invite those concerned to apply to the Somerville Press Ltd for proper acknowledgement.

PICTURE CREDITS

P. 19. *Candida Lycett Green (left) unveiling a plaque commemorating her father, John Betjeman, at Marylebone Station in 2006.* Released into public domain by the copyright holder.

P. 24. *Gormanston Castle, Co. Meath.* (JIM FITZPATRICK) Licensed under the Creative Commons Attribution 2.0 Generic Licence.

P. 26. *Jammet's Hotel and Restaurant, St Andrew's Street, circa 1900 -1920.* (FERGUS O'CONNOR COLLECTION, NATIONAL LIBRARY OF IRELAND) Licensed by National Library of Ireland on The Commons. No known copyright restrictions.

P. 29. *W.H. Auden* (CARL VAN VECHTEN PHOTOGRAPHS COLLECTION, LIBRARY OF CONGRESS) Public Domain. According to the library, there are no known copyright restrictions on the use of this work.

P. 34. *Clandeboye* (ROBERT FRENCH, LAWRENCE PHOTOGRAPH COLLECTION, NATIONAL LIBRARY OF IRELAND) No known copyright restrictions.

P. 36. *Dungarvan* (MIK HERMAN) – Licensed under the Creative Commons Attribution-Share-Alike 3.0 Unported licence.

P. 45. *Field Marshal Sir Philip Chetwode* (JOHN ST HELIER LANDER) Public Domain from Wikimedia Commons.

P. 55. *Lady Elizabeth Cavendish* (LUCIAN FREUD) Bridgeman Images.

P. 64. *Éamon de Valera* (NATIONAL PHOTO COMPANY COLLECTION – UNITED STATES LIBRARY OF CONGRESS) Public Domain from Wikimedia Commons. This work is from the National Photo collection at the Library of Congress. No known copyright restrictions on the use of this work.

P. 69. *Sir John Maffey, later Lord Rugby* (PHOTOGRAPHER UNKNOWN – NATIONAL PORTRAIT GALLERY, LONDON) Public Domain from Wikimedia Commons.

P. 72. *William Joyce, Lord Haw Haw* (BERT HARDY) From Wikimedia Commons. This work created by the United Kingdom Government is in the public domain.

P. 78. *Sir Laurence Olivier* (ALLEN WARREN) From Wikimedia Commons. Licensed under the Creative Commons Attribution Share Alike 3.0 Unported licence.

P. 80. *Powerscourt House, County Wicklow* (AMANDA SUSAN MUNROE) From Wikimedia Commons. Licensed under the Creative Commons Attribution Share Alike 3.0 Unported license.

P. 83. *Seán O'Faoláin* (HOWARD COSTER, NATIONAL PORTRAIT GALLERY, LONDON) From Wikimedia Commons. Licenced under the Creative Commons Attribution-Share-Alike-4.0 International licence.

P. 96. *Patrick Kavanagh* (ELINOR WILTSHIRE, NATIONAL LIBRARY OF IRELAND) Public Domain. Released by the NLI. No known copyright restrictions.

P. 99. *John Charles McQuaid Archbishop of Dublin.* Licensed under the Creative Commons Attribution Share Alike 4.0 International licence.

P. 104. *Lismore Castle* From Wikimedia Commons This file is licensed under the Creative Commons Attribution Share Alike 2.5 Generic licence.

P. 107. *William Cecil James Philip John Paul Howard Clonmore, 8th Earl of Wicklow* (BASSANO LIMITED) Public Domain from Wikimedia Commons.

P. 116. *Fair Day in Dungarvan* (ROBERT FRENCH, LAWRENCE PHOTOGRAPH COLLECTION, NATIONAL LIBRARY OF IRELAND) Public Domain. No known copyright restrictions.

P. 131. *Tullynally Castle* (PETER GAVIGAN) Licenced under the Creative Commons Attribution Share Alike 3.0 Unported, 2.5 Generic, 2.0 Generic and 1.0 Generic Licence.

P. 132. *Evelyn Waugh* (CARL VAN VECHTEN) Public Domain. This work is from the Carl Van Vechten Photographs collection at the Library of Congress. According to the library, there are no known copyright restrictions on the use of this work.

P. 138. *Siegfried Sassoon* (GEORGE CHARLES BERESFORD) Public Domain in its country of origin and other countries and areas where the copyright term is the author's life plus 70 years or fewer.

P. 150. *Lord Alfred Douglas* (GEORGE CHARLES BERESFORD) Public Domain from Wikimedia Commons.

FRONT COVER IMAGE: *Betjeman statue at St. Pancras Station by sculptor Martin Jennings.* Licensed under the Creative Commons Attribution-Share Alike 3.0 Unported licence.

BACK COVER IMAGE: *John Betjeman* (Daily Herald Archive at National Media Museum) Public Domain. No known copyright restrictions

Printed in Great Britain
by Amazon